PETER FRYER
BLACK P
IN THE BR
EMPIRE
D0538030
DISCARDED
FROM
RICHMOND UPON THAMES
LIBRARY SERVICE

PETER FRYER

BLACK PEOPLE IN THE BRITISH EMPIRE

First published 1988 by Pluto Press
345 Archway Road, London N6 5AA
and 1436 West Randolph, Chicago,
Illinois 60607, USA

This edition published 1989
Republished as a Pluto Classic 1993

Copyright © Peter Fryer, 1988, 1989
All rights reserved.
The right of Peter Fryer to be identified as the author
of this work has been asserted by him in accordance with
the Copyright, Designs and Patents Act 1988.

ISBN 0 7453 0342 0

A catalogue record for this book is available
from the British Library

Impression : 99 98 97 96 9 8 7 6 5 4 3

Printed in the EC by The Ipswich Book Co. Ltd

Contents

The present is where we get lost –
if we forget our past and have
no vision of the future.
Ayi Kwei Armah, *The Healers* (1978)

Preface

The present book is intended to be complementary to my *Staying Power: The History of Black People in Britain* (1984). Ideally it should be read first, since it describes, in greater detail than was possible or appropriate in the earlier book, the long history of overseas exploitation, oppression and 'underdevelopment' by British capitalism of which the black presence in metropolitan Britain has been one result. There may seem to be some overlap between the two books but in fact there is very little. And, where there is, I have taken the opportunity to correct errors of fact and emphasis in *Staying Power* and to supplement that book with further material (specifically, on London as a slave port, on the role of India in the funding of the industrial revolution, and on the racist bias of nineteenth-century British historiography). In order not to make the present book too bulky I have confined the account of black resistance to that in the Caribbean and the Indian sub-continent, those parts of the British Empire of greatest interest to British-born black readers, whose parents mostly came from one or other of those areas. Readers particularly interested in Africa, Tasmania, Australia or New Zealand under British rule will find here some account of that rule, but will have to look elsewhere for an account of the resistance to it. After all, this is only an introduction. Like its predecessor, however, this book is not intended solely for black readers. As the Introduction argues, white people in Britain also need to know something about black history, without which British history is seriously incomplete. For black people have played, not a peripheral, but a central part in British history. Until quite recently their contribution has not been properly acknowledged; and even now most white people in Britain are unaware of it.

It gives me much pleasure to thank Anna Grimshaw and Rozina Visram for their kindness in reading and commenting on an early draft. I am grateful to Charlie Brandt, James Fryer and Geoff Pilling for a variety of technical help. Many other people have contributed ideas and cogent criticisms of *Staying Power*. Of these I should like to give special thanks to Christopher Fyfe: I have profited greatly from the thoughtful material he has been kind enough to send me. A number of students in various institutions of learning have, during the past four years, heard my lectures on some of the topics treated in this book. Their questions have frequently stimulated me to fresh thought and further research, and those of them who chance to pick up this book will find some of our discussions shadowed in its pages. Lastly, I am grateful to Frances Fryer and Raymond McCaffrey for introducing me to the novel from which the epigraph is taken, and to Emily Fryer Moreira and Luíz Moreira de Souza for their patience and encouragement.

Introduction

This is a book about some aspects of British imperial history. It is mainly about Africans, Asians, and people of African and Asian descent under British rule. There is also something in it about Tasmanians, black Australians ('Aborigines'), and Maoris.

A white person who writes on any aspect of black history must answer the question: what has black history got to do with white people? This is a political question. It is a question about power and how power is distributed or, more precisely, polarized, in the society we live in. Failure to face and answer this question suggests ignorance, incompetence, or bad faith.

Some white people in Britain have much more power than is good for them, or for the rest of us. But no black person has any real power at all, even if he or she wears a police uniform or sits in parliament. The very word 'race', which geneticists and anthropologists have discarded as meaningless, survives merely as a political category. In Britain, as in South Africa, racial labels survive as devices to shut out a section of the population from power, to make them into second-class citizens.

There has been a continuous black presence in Britain for 500 years. All that time, some white people have had all the power in their own hands and no black person has had any power at all, save of the most token kind. And white historians, almost without exception, have done their best to deprive black people of their history, too. They have consistently belittled or wiped out the black past – which is essentially just another way of depriving black people of power. 'There is no more significant pointer to the character of a society', observed E. H. Carr, 'than the kind of history it writes *or fails to write*.'[1] It follows that there is no more significant pointer to the character of British society than the exclusion of black people from our history books.

It is hardly surprising that serious students of black history have tended to view white writers on the subject with misgivings. In the United States, many students have seen the chief purpose of black historiography as the encouragement of black pride and a feeling of personal worth; this is obviously not the business of white writers. Yet there are in the United States black historians who are saying, with Benjamin Quarles, that 'black history is no longer a matter of limited concern', that white people too need to know black history, since for them it provides 'a new version of American history, one that especially challenges our national sense of smugness and self-righteousness and our avowal of fair play'.[2] Many other eminent American historians, white as well as black, agree. 'We cannot understand America', writes Walter Metzger, 'without the help of those studies now called "black".'[3] 'The history of America', writes Eugene Genovese, 'can no longer be written without a full account of its black element, [which] penetrates and has been penetrated by everything else.'[4]

These statements apply with no less force to Britain and British history. Here too white people need to know something about black history, since for us it furnishes a version of British history that strongly challenges *our* national sense of smugness and self-righteousness, *our* avowal of fair play. Like American history, British history cannot be written honestly without taking into account the contribution that black people have made to it. The past that historians study is not a dead past. It has shaped the present and lives on in the present. By understanding the past, wrote R. G. Collingwood, 'we incorporate it into our present thought, and enable ourselves ... to use that heritage for our own advancement'.[5] Without knowing something about black history we can neither understand the world of today nor see the way forward to the world of tomorrow.

The sort of history taught in British schools and universities has traditionally been the history of people with power. In schools, until quite recently, it was mainly a chronicle of kings and queens, national saviours, heroes and heroines, great statesmen, great leaders in peace and war.[6] The history of the powerless, though these have always been the great majority, was largely ignored. Yet the official version of our history labels itself as 'patriotic'. It is more accurately described as conservative, nationalist, and racist.

In 1899 a former headmaster of Harrow public school, whose task had been to train the sons of the ruling class, summed up his duties in these words:

> An English Head-master, as he looks to the future of his pupils, will not forget that they are destined to be the citizens of the greatest empire under heaven; he will teach them patriotism ... he will inspire them with faith in the divinely ordered mission of their country and their race.[7]

Britain's 'relentless pursuit of its own selfish ends' is, in the official version of our history, 'smugly identified with service to mankind at large'. Englishmen's deeds are glorified and ulterior motives are attributed to everybody else.[8] Thus A. P. Newton, celebrating *A Hundred Years of the British Empire* (1940), claimed that 'the other empires of history were mainly founded by military force, but during the last three centuries ... the British Empire has been expanded far beyond the limits of the United Kingdom, not, mainly, by conquest, ... but by wholly peaceful means.'[9] David Thomson declared in 1950, in the eighth volume of the Pelican History of England, that 'British imperialism ... was never racialist'; on the other hand, 'other contemporary imperialisms *were* racialist'.[10] And A. P. Thornton, in *The Imperial Idea and its Enemies* (1959), asserted that 'English patriotism has never been racial'.[11]

The essential racism of the official version of our history is seen above all in its glorification of the British Empire and its arrogant attitude to those who were that empire's subjects. Throughout the empire, and here in Britain too, black people's history has been the precise opposite of the official myths. By disguising or glorifying the true history of colonialism,* and by writing black people out of British history, the official historians have marginalized and thus further oppressed those whose history they have distorted or concealed. Their distortions and omissions have had the clear purpose of maintaining the existing power structure. This purpose has governed the historians' method, choice of materials, and interpretation of those materials.

In recent years a number of historians and history teachers have begun to challenge the official version. They have refused to leave the powerless, the labouring majority, out of the picture any longer. The modest amount of people's history, or history from below, that is taught in British schools has displeased Margaret Thatcher and her friends. They want our children to be taught to see the past record of the British ruling class in the mellowest possible light. Not long before she became prime minister, Thatcher wrote, in a pamphlet published by the Centre for Policy Studies, that 'a whole generation has been brought up to misunderstand and denigrate our national history', that 'our population has been indoctrinated with considerable folly', so that 'they are quite unaware that the Britain of the eighteenth and nineteenth centuries was admired and envied the world over for its liberty, for the comparative well-being of its inhabitants, for achievements in ... manufacturing, for its subjects' enterprise, patriotism and social conscience'.[13] And, as prime minister, Thatcher has sought to ensure that the history taught in our schools should project what *The Times Higher*

* Colonialism is used here to mean the economic, political and cultural domination by Europeans of others.[12]

Education Supplement has called 'an interpretation of the British experience that is expedient to our present leaders rather than faithful to the historical record'.[14] Periodically, from the chair of the Centre for Policy Studies, Thatcher's 'historian-adviser', Lord Thomas of Swynnerton, otherwise known as Hugh Thomas, has demanded a more 'patriotic' orientation in history teaching.[15]

Sir Keith Joseph, while secretary of state for education, was more specific. On 23 August 1984 he told a conference of American historians that 'pride in one's country and its achievements' should be fostered in schools. He added this guideline: 'The teacher should lead the pupil towards his or her own decisions about which aspects of national events, institutions, or culture, are most deserving of admiration.'[16]

This is an excellent guideline, given one essential precondition: that the black contribution to British history, long neglected in syllabuses and textbooks, shall now be included – in other words, that Britain's black population shall no longer be denied a past.

This implies that pupils, black and white alike, shall have access to facts and topics that have not hitherto been familiar to them. Those who are to make their 'own decisions' about what and what not to admire in British history, should know of the part played by black labour – in the Caribbean and in India – to the growth of Britain's wealth and major industries and cities. They should be told how and on what basis British racism arose, and what its role has been in the validation of colonialism. They should be told that black people did not start coming to Britain after the Second World War but that their presence here goes back some 2,000 years and has been continuous since the beginning of the sixteenth century or earlier. They should be told that, just as Britain's black slaves in the Caribbean resisted plantation servitude, so the black slaves here in Britain freed themselves as individuals by running away from domestic servitude. They should be told of the contributions made by black radicals to the building of the British labour movement and the winning of civil liberties in this country. Not least, pupils should be told of the thousands of black soldiers and sailors who, fighting under the Union Jack, were wounded, crippled for life, or killed in battle.[17]

These and other aspects of British black history include achievements gained in the teeth of unremitting race prejudice, consistent racial discrimination, and murderous racist attacks. Such achievements are surely, to use Sir Keith Joseph's words, 'deserving of admiration'. So it is the duty of teachers who recognize the need to combat racism to take Joseph at his word by throwing light on this hitherto obscure area of British history. For how can people make their own decisions about what is admirable in British history if they do not have free access to the facts?

British black history must now begin to take its rightful place within the school curriculum, as an essential part of the history of this country's poor and labouring majority as well as a central part of British imperial history. Giving it that rightful place is a task which faces both black and white educators. It is a task they have to shoulder together.

Part I
How Britain Became 'Great Britain'

1
Britain and its Empire

British history cannot be understood in isolation. To make sense of what has happened in this country we have to study the histories of four other areas as well: Ireland; the Caribbean; the Indian sub-continent; and Africa. It was in those areas that the British ruling classes made their fortune and founded their empire.

England's rulers served an apprenticeship in colonialism from the twelfth century onwards. They did so in Ireland, where they learnt how to conquer, rule and rob other nations. In 1172 King Henry II, self-styled Lord of Ireland, shared out his newly conquered Irish territories among his leading followers and turned Dublin and the area around it into a special dependency of the English Crown. This area, surrounded by a palisade, was later known as the English Pale. Only those Irish people willing to become English in speech, dress and appearance were permitted to live there. The rest were hunted down and exterminated like vermin. So fierce was their resistance that in the early seventeenth century the English thought Ireland was as 'savage' as Virginia, and English military maps of Ireland were being produced in great numbers.[1]

Before the English invasion Ireland had been one of western Europe's richest and most advanced countries. As England's first overseas colony it was transformed into one of the poorest and most backward. In this, as in most other respects, it was the prototype of British colonialism.

But when Britain's merchant capitalists, challenging their more advanced European rivals, set themselves the aim of amassing as much wealth as possible, conquest took second place to trade. Lewes Roberts, a director of the East India Company, explained in *The Treasure of Traffike* (1641) how his class was enriching itself: 'It is not our conquests, but our Commerce; it is not our swords, but our sayls.'[2] Roberts was writing at the very dawn of the triangular trade, perhaps the most lucrative commerce of all. It was gradually being discovered that huge profits could be made from buying Africans, shipping them to the Caribbean, and setting them to work under the whip to produce sugar for sale in England. This was the earliest form of exploitation of black labour. In the second half of the eighteenth century the plunder of Bengal provided British capitalism with a further massive transfusion of wealth at the expense of black people.

There has been much controversy about these two transfusions of wealth and how important they were to the industrialization of Britain. What cannot be denied is that they came at the critical time. Britain's industrial revolution benefited from what one historian describes as an 'assisted take-off'.[3] Another calls the earliest forms of exploitation of black people – slavery and plunder – a 'special forced draught' which was 'probably decisive for the British cotton industry, the real industrial pioneer' and gave Britain's capitalists 'several precious decades of dizzy economic expansion from which they drew inestimable benefits'.[4] A third historian has summed up these benefits as follows:

> Our possession of the West Indies, like that of India ... gave us the strength, the support, but especially the capital, the wealth, at a time when no other European nation possessed such a reserve, which enabled us to come through the great struggle of the Napoleonic Wars, the keen competition of the eighteenth and nineteenth centuries, and enabled us ... to lay the foundation of that commercial and financial leadership which ... enabled us to make our great position in the world.[5]

Those were the words of Winston Churchill, addressing a banquet of West Indies sugar planters in London on 20 July 1939.

Thus the history of Britain and the history of the British Empire are two sides of the same coin. Neither can be understood without the other. And at the heart of their unity, interpenetration, and interdependence is the age-old black presence in Britain. That presence was the direct result of those two 'special forced draughts' which, above all else, put the 'Great' into Great Britain. Sugar planters from the West Indies and 'nabobs' from India, returning to Britain to enjoy their new wealth, brought with them their retinues of black household servants. By the second half of the eighteenth century Britain's black population numbered about 10,000 – living witnesses to British capitalism's oppression and exploitation of black people in the Caribbean and India.

2
The Triangular Trade

Just before the Second World War the young Trinidadian scholar Eric Williams completed his doctoral dissertation on 'The Economic Aspect of the Abolition of the British West Indian Slave Trade and Slavery', a topic suggested to him by his countryman C. L. R. James. Hoping to have it published, he took the typescript to one of the most progressive publishers of the day, who handed it back to him with the words: 'I would never publish such a book. It is contrary to the British tradition.'[1] Challenging the British official tradition has never been easy. Williams's book was published in the United States in 1944, under the title *Capitalism & Slavery*. But it was not to be published here in Britain for another 20 years.

Capitalism & Slavery caused much embarrassment to historians working within the official tradition, who had written 'almost as if Britain had introduced Negro slavery solely for the satisfaction of abolishing it'.[2] It is fashionable nowadays to say that Williams's work is discredited. The truth is far more complex. To be sure, many details have needed correction in the light of later research; of what historical work published 40 years ago can that not be said? Referring to Williams's thesis that the slave trade and slavery were abolished for basically economic reasons, Christopher Fyfe admits that critics have skilfully unscrewed the nuts and bolts. He adds: 'Still one wonders – has the edifice really fallen? Certainly it has not yet been replaced.'[3] Williams's thesis that the profits from the triangular trade became a major factor in the accumulation of capital necessary for industrialization has never been refuted – though another major factor, wealth obtained from the plunder of India, must also be taken into account (see pp. 17–20 below). One of the main difficulties in quantifying the multiple profits of the triangular trade is that there are large gaps in the records. As Donald Woodward has pointed out, 'for the long-distance triangular trades the Port Books are particularly deficient and seriously understate the level of British trade. This is especially true of such trades as ... the slave trade'.[4] What has to be kept in mind is the close economic unity of Britain and its Caribbean colonies in the

eighteenth century. Restating his thesis in a 1969 lecture, Williams showed how:
1) The fortunes of eighteenth-century Britain were greatly influenced by the plantation economy of the West Indies;
2) In turn, economic, political and intellectual developments in Britain had profound effects in shaping the course of West Indian history;
3) Above all, Britain's Caribbean colonies, created by the mercantilist system to serve its ends, 'always remained firmly integrated into the British metropolitan economy. The capital was British; decision-making took place in Britain ... *The economies of the sugar islands ... remained an integral part ... of the British economy.*'[5]

Moreover, as Richard B. Sheridan has made clear, an adequate analysis of the industrial revolution entails a consideration of 'a whole trading area of economic interactions'. The Atlantic was the most dynamic trading area and, outside Britain itself, 'the most important element in the growth of this area in the century or more prior to 1776 was the slave-plantation, particularly of the cane sugar variety in the islands of the Caribbean Sea.'[6]

The British West Indies were a single-crop economy, and that crop was sugar, the 'white gold' of the New World. Barbados began exporting sugar in 1646; by 1660 St Kitts was exporting more sugar than indigo; Jamaica started planting sugar in 1664. Tobacco, cotton, ginger, cocoa and coffee were also grown but were of comparatively minor importance. Sugar was king, and its rule was never challenged.[7]

In order to grow sugar, British planters in the Caribbean needed two things. First of all, they needed virtually unlimited long-term credit to sustain them during the years it took to grow a first crop and to 'season' the labour. Such credit was their life-blood, and it was provided by commission agents, or 'factors', in the City of London. These commission agents put up the money for the purchase of plantations and slaves, and made their fortunes on the interest they charged. They became in effect the planters' bankers. These were the fat spiders at the centre of the whole web: men like the City aldermen Sir John Bawden, Sir John Eyles, and Sir Francis Eyles – and Henry Lascelles, MP, who sucked so much wealth from the commission system, from sugar, and from outright fraud, that his successors became earls of Harewood. This credit system primed the pump, and did so very profitably indeed.

The second thing the planters needed was cheap labour to plant and tend the crops, cut the canes and process the sugar. After a brief experiment with indentured English convicts, they found the labour they needed in Africa. As *The Cambridge History of the British Empire* tells us, the African slave trade became 'the very foundation of West

Indian prosperity'.[8] To pay for slaves, Britain's manufacturing industries sent their products to the African coast. They sent textiles made in Lancashire, guns and wrought-iron goods made in Birmingham, brass goods made in Bristol, copper goods made in Swansea, Flint and Lancashire, pewter made in Liverpool, and cutlery made in Sheffield. With these products went gunpowder, bullets, tallow, tobacco-pipes, glass beads, toys, malt spirits, and beer from the Whitbread and Truman breweries – 'very little that is not of our own growth and manufacture', observed a writer in 1763,[9] though re-exports did include Indian textiles and Swedish iron. According to one contemporary source, the yearly value of British manufactured goods exported to Africa soared from £83,000 in 1710 to £401,000 in 1787.[10] These goods were bartered for human beings on what was then known as the Guinea Coast.

'Guinea' was soon the popular name for the new gold coin struck in 1663 by a slave-trading company called the Royal Adventurers into Africa, whose stockholders 'included every major figure in the Court and in the Administration, as well as every moneyed man in London and Bristol'.[11] For 200 years real English wealth, the sort of wealth that went with high rank and social prestige, would be measured in guineas, which is to say 'Africas'. Some of the earliest guineas bore on the obverse, below the bust of King Charles II in profile, a tiny African elephant. In Liverpool, soon to become Europe's major slaving port, the City fathers were less squeamish: when they built a new town hall in the mid-eighteenth century they decorated it with the heads, carved in stone, of African elephants and African slaves.

The role of Liverpool and Bristol in the slave trade, and the decisive contribution it made to their growth and prosperity throughout the eighteenth century, are well known. Less well known is how early Bristol entered the trade. There is now enough evidence to prove conclusively that the trade became 'of prime importance' to Bristol soon after 1630;[12] so that by 1713 the mayor was calling it 'one of the great supports of our people'.[13] In the eighteenth-century roll-call of British cities, the trade in slaves and the trade in slave-produced sugar together made Bristol second only to London.[14]

Hardly known at all is the part played by London in the eighteenth-century slave trade. Between 1672 and 1713, as is generally recognized, the Royal African Company, successor to the short-lived Royal Adventurers, sent more than 500 ships on the triangular voyage. These ships carried goods worth £1,500,000 and took on board about 125,000 Africans, of whom about 100,000 were landed alive in the New World.[15] At the peak of its activities the company was shipping Africans at the rate of about 5,000 a year.[16] All historians without exception have gravely underestimated London's share in later eighteenth-century slaving ventures. Even Eric Williams failed to question the accepted view that the London slave trade greatly and permanently declined after 1720. 'There is abundant proof to the contrary', writes James A. Rawley, who has begun to set London's later record straight. From 1698 to 1807, more than 2,500 slavers left the port for Africa – 'an astonishing figure ... in the light of what some historians have argued'. London was the leading English slaving port until the late 1720s; it continued as a slaving port until the legal trade ended; its activity was reduced from 1730 to the late 1750s, but it experienced a resurgence in the 1760s and 1770s; and in the last years of the legal trade it ranked as England's second most important slaving port.[17]

But it wasn't only the three big slaving ports that prospered. The industries producing the goods with which the slaves were bought, and the cities associated with those industries, prospered too. The 'opulence' of Manchester, as well as that of Liverpool, was admitted in 1841 to be 'as really owing to the toil and suffering of the negro, as if his hands had excavated their docks and fabricated their steam-engines'.[18] The slave trade was one of the 'powerful factors influencing the early success' of the Birmingham gun trade.[19] The slave trade gave the Swansea copper industry such a 'special forced draught' that by the middle of the nineteenth century it was supplying over half the copper needs of the entire world.[20] Copper production had been especially boosted by the practice of copper-sheathing ships' hulls, an innovation first adopted by Britain's slaving fleet. Other industries, too, benefited directly from the slave trade: shipbuilding, for instance, and its ancillary industries sailmaking and ropemaking. In 1774 there were 15 roperies in Liverpool, and in 1788 it was estimated that 'the Artificers and Mechanics' employed in the port received £100,000 a year for the labour and materials used in equipping slave-ships.[21]

British traders bought slaves in Africa not only for resale to British planters in the Caribbean, and in the North American colonies, but also for sale to Spanish colonists in the New World. Spain was the only colonizing power that lacked any kind of base on the West African coast. So the Spaniards had to turn to middlemen for their supply of slaves. And the English were happy to oblige. The first licence to Spaniards to buy slaves in the 'Caribbees' and Jamaica was granted as early as 1663, and the traffic 'continued spasmodically' for the next 50 years.[22] Then in 1713, under the treaty of Utrecht, Britain acquired the *assiento*, the official contract to supply 4,800 Africans a year to south and central America, the Spanish West Indies, Mexico and Florida. Until 1791, a quarter of the Atlantic slave trade was in British hands, and from 1791 to 1806 Britain's share was over half.

Two questions are often asked about the slave trade. First, how many Africans were transported? Second, what monetary profits were made from the trade, in particular by Britain? These questions are hard to answer with any degree of precision; as more and more research is done the estimates are constantly being revised. The best guide here is the late Walter Rodney. On the first question, he has this to say:

> Any figure of Africans imported into the Americas which is narrowly based on the surviving records is bound to be low, because there were so many people at the time who had a vested interest in smuggling slaves (and withholding data) ...
>
> On any basic figure of Africans landed alive in the Americas, one would have to make several extensions – starting with a calculation to cover mortality in transhipment ... The resultant figure would be many times the millions landed alive outside of Africa, and it is that figure which represents the number of Africans directly removed from the population and labour force of Africa.[23]

Rodney suggests that more than 15 million Africans were landed alive and that, between 1445 and 1870, Africa lost altogether 40–50 million of its population as a result of the slave trade and associated activities.[24]

The most recent estimate of the profit made by British slave-merchants on the sale of the 2,500,000 Africans they are thought to have handled between 1630 and 1807 puts it at about £12 million.[25] As Rodney says, 'the actual dimensions are not easy to fix, but the profits were fabulous'.[26] And, as will be seen, these 'fabulous' profits were merely a fraction of the wealth generated by the triangular trade as a whole.

Not all the Africans involved in the slave trade were victims. (Black slaves were never *merely* victims; as we shall see later, they resisted servitude with all their might and fought back against their oppressors.) Nor were Europeans all villains, or the only villains. Some Europeans raised their voices against the trade, though they did not begin to do so in Britain until the second half of the eighteenth century, by which time it had been under way for some 200 years. Many African rulers and merchants collaborated with the European slave-dealers by selling fellow Africans to them for transportation. The Europeans took full advantage of divisions among African states, some of which they bribed and incited to make war on their neighbours, and even to kidnap their own subjects, so as to be able to sell the captives into slavery. Once the trade in slaves had been started in any given part of Africa, 'it was beyond the capacity of any given African state to change the situation.'[27] Some African states took up slave-raiding in self-protection, since the European guns supplied to their belligerent neighbours could be bought only with slaves.

> Rapine and plunder, organized man-hunts, kidnapping that bred more kidnapping, deterioration in the customary law – all these lay behind the facade of relatively orderly and peaceful agreements between European slavers and coastal chiefs ... The rulers benefited ... by receiving the best cloth, drinking the most alcohol, and preserving the widest collection of durable items for prestige purposes. It is this factor of realized self-interest which goes some way towards explaining the otherwise incomprehensible actions of Africans towards Africans.[28]

It is often suggested that the Europeans merely took over and adapted to their own purposes a pre-existing system of slavery. This is a misleading over-simplification. Before the coming of the Europeans the institution of slavery was not widespread in Africa. Forms of production, class relationships, and forms of state varied very much from region to region and in many areas servitude resembled what in Europe was known as serfdom or villeinage rather than what is generally understood as slavery.[29] Walter Rodney pointed out in his *History of the Upper Guinea Coast* (1970) that the so-called 'domestic slaves' of West Africa could not be sold, except for serious offences. They had their own plots of land and/or a right to a proportion of the fruits of their labour. They could marry, and their children had rights of inheritance. They could rise to positions of great trust.[30] Clearly there is a great differerence between this form of servitude and the plantation slavery practised in the Caribbean.

The Africans bought by the European slave-traders were mostly very young: healthy, able-bodied young men and women between the ages of 15 and 25. Cargoes often included a proportion of children, but people over the age of 30 were almost always rejected. The young men, young women and children were branded like cattle, then carried across the Atlantic, the men chained in the hold for 20 hours out of the 24. Of those transported in British ships, between one in four and one in twelve perished on the way. It was taken for granted that, of those who survived the 'middle passage', one in three would die, of dysentery or suicide (a form of resistance) in their first three years in the New World. Those first three years were the 'seasoning' or acclimatization period. The survivors were set to work under the whip to produce 'white gold' for their white masters. Flogging – in Jamaica, with a 10ft cart-whip – was routine punishment for almost every offence, and was inflicted on girls, women, boys and men alike.[31] The slaves were grossly underfed, as both an economy and an attempt, rarely successful, to break their spirit.

From the forced labour of those millions of Africans in the sugar plantations, millions of pounds were made, over a period not far short of 200 years. Britain's sugar imports from the Caribbean trebled between 1700 and 1764.[32] For Britain, wrote Frank Wesley Pitman, this brought 'perhaps ... the greatest increment of wealth in modern times'.[33] Michael Craton has calculated that 'over the entire period of slavery the West Indian plantations alone may have brought the planters an aggregate profit of over £150,000,000, at a rate that averaged £1,000,000 a year throughout the eighteenth century.' Taking the triangular trade as a whole, he adds that 'between 1640 and 1838 private English individuals and concerns interested in slavery may have generated as much as £450 millions in profits: two thirds of it in the eighteenth century and half in the half century after 1750.'[34]

What happened to the profits? Some were squandered on luxurious living by the absentee planters who came back to Britain with their black household slaves. Here was 'a West India aristocracy of great wealth and political power'.[35] Absentee proprietorship was rife on all the islands from the very beginning of colonization.[36] Take Antigua: at least 52 of its planter families had members away from the island for long periods in the years 1730–75; they included 20 London–West India merchants, 12 MPs, 9 titled persons, and one Lord Mayor of London.[37] Jamaica in 1774 was said to have 2,000 absentees, to whom three-quarters of the island's land and slaves belonged.[38] The 'West Indians' lived in a grand and ostentatious style – though John Gardner Kemeys was clearly exaggerating when he wrote in 1783 that 'near half the wealth of the Colonies is prodigally spent in London in luxuries and follies'.[39]

Some of the profits were used to finance the pro-slavery West India lobby, probably the first organized parliamentary lobby in history. This was the powerful lever by which the 'West Indians' exercised an influence on British politics, on the law-making process, on the administration of justice and, through the press, on public opinion. The lobby's strength became 'a dominant factor in the control of colonial policy'.[40]

Some of the profits were reinvested in the colonial trade – were used, that is, to buy the manufactured goods needed to run the plantations.

Here was a further boost for British industry. E. J. Hobsbawm writes of this 'rising demand for European goods in the plantations' that by 1700 something like 20 per cent of English exports may have gone to colonial areas (including the colonies of other European powers); that in 1759–60 and 1770 over one-third went to British colonies alone (not counting direct exports to colonies of Spain and Portugal); and that in 1784 no less than half of Britain's exports went to the colonies (including the recently independent United States).[41] Well might John Oldmixon boast of Barbados in 1708: 'When we examine the Riches that have been rais'd by the Produce of this little Spot of Ground, we shall find that it has been as good as a Mine of Silver or Gold to the Crown of *England*.'[42]

Lastly, some of the profits were invested directly in British industry. The coal and iron industries of south Wales depended directly on the triangular trade for their initial funding. In 1765 Anthony Bacon MP was granted a contract to furnish 'seasoned, able and working negroes' to the islands of Grenada, the Grenadines, Tobago, St Vincent, and Dominica, and the government paid him almost £67,000 for these slaves. The money went straight into industrial development around Merthyr Tydfil, then a mere hamlet. Bacon took a 99-year lease on 4,000 acres of virgin mineral land, developed iron-foundries and coalmines that came to be known as 'Bacon's mineral kingdom', turned the Cyfarthfa ironworks into 'the largest munition works yet established on the coalfield', and made his fortune in the process.[43] Thomas Harris, a Bristol slave-merchant with interests in the sugar industry, bought an interest in the Dowlais ironworks, Cyfarthfa's neighbouring and rival enterprise, in 1768. Fifty years later Dowlais was Merthyr Tydfil's third largest ironworks.[44]

The north Wales slate industry, producing roofing slates for factory workers' dwellings, was financed by profits from the triangular trade. Richard Pennant MP, first Baron Penrhyn, who inherited the largest estate in Jamaica, devoted his plantation's profits to the development of the Penrhyn slate quarries, the building of roads and, in 1790, the construction of the harbour of Port Penrhyn, near Bangor.[45]

The south Yorkshire iron industry, the Liverpool and Manchester Railway, the Great Western Railway and the original steam engine of James Watt were all financed in part with profits accumulated from the triangular trade. The early history of the British banking system, from the first country banks and Barclays right up to the Bank of England, is closely connected with the triangular trade, as is the early history of British insurance.

At the time, they made no bones about it. In contemporary books and pamphlets slave trade and sugar trade 'are treated as inseparably connected, and as forming together the foundation of English greatness'.[46] The Royal African Company's chief agent on the West African coast wrote in 1690 that 'the Kingdoms Pleasure, Glory, and Grandure' were more advanced by the sugar produced by black slaves 'than by any other Commodity we deal in or produce, Wooll not excepted'.[47] It was common knowledge, wrote the anonymous author of *The Importance of the Sugar Colonies to Great-Britain* (1731), 'that our Sugar Colonies are of the greatest Consequence and Advantage to the Trade and Navigation of *Great-Britain*'.[48] It was common knowledge, too, that 'the very Existence and Preservation of the Sugar Colonies depend upon the *British* trade to *Africa*': that was how planters and merchants put it in a 1749 petition to the House of Commons.[49] The Royal African Company's surgeon wrote in 1725 that the slave trade was

> a glorious and advantageous Trade ... the Hinge on which all the Trade of this Globe moves ... for ... put a Stop to the Slave Trade, and all the others cease of Course ... who sweetens the Ladies Tea, and the generous Bowl [i.e. rum punch]; and who reaps the Profit of all? Therefore, let every true *Briton* unanimously join to concert Measures, how to center this advantageous Trade in *England*.[50]

Referring in 1763 to 'these so necessary *Negro* slaves', John Campbell reflected on 'what an amazing variety of trades receive their daily support, as many of them originally did their being, from the calls of the *African* and *West India* markets'. The profit arising from the sale of slaves 'and every other accession of gain, from whatever article produced, centers ultimately here, and becomes the property of the inhabitants of *Britain*'.[51] Robert Norris of Liverpool wrote in 1788 that the slave trade, 'connected as it is with the West Indian Commerce ... is of the utmost Consequence to the employment of many thousands of our Fellow-subjects, to the Naval Power of Britain, and to the Royal Revenues'.[52]

There were, to be sure, defenders of the slave trade whose thoughts on the subject were tinged with humanitarian scruples. Writing in 1764, John Hippisley, who believed that Africa could supply 'millions more, and go on doing the same to the end of time', found the trade absolutely necessary but urged the slave-owners to treat their slaves as well as they possibly could:

> The impossibility of doing without slaves in the West-Indies will always prevent this traffick being dropped. The necessity, the absolute necessity, then, of carrying it on, must, since there is no other,

> be its excuse ... Sensibility, and deep reflection upon their sad state, do not operate very powerfully among the negroes; yet they are not *totally* devoid of them ... [Let] the white possessors ... soften the misery of their condition by every safe and reasonable indulgence that their humanity can suggest, and that the nature of the case will admit.[53]

It should be borne in mind that sugar production, in Sheridan's words, 'was more demanding of hard physical labour and more destructive to life and limb than that of most other tropical and semi-tropical staples'.[54] For instance, the labour force had to undertake the entire task of preparing the land for planting; the land was not ploughed, but holed laboriously with the hoe, a task that imposed a heavy physical strain. Sheridan's observation is true also of the industrial sector of sugar production. In 1802 Lady Nugent, wife of Jamaica's lieutenant-governor, wrote in her journal after a visit to a sugar mill:

> I asked the overseer how often his people were relieved. He said every twelve hours; but how dreadful to think of their standing twelve hours over a boiling cauldron ... and he owned to me that sometimes they did fall asleep, and got their poor fingers into the mill; and he shewed me a hatchet, that was always ready to sever the whole limb, as the only means of saving the poor sufferer's life![55]

To the planters, the slaves were essentially 'a form of capital equipment',[56] more easily and more cheaply replaceable than machinery. So it was more cost-effective to chop off a finger, hand or arm than to stop the machinery for as long as it took to set a trapped sugar-boiler free.

Nor was it only in Cuba, under Spanish masters, that black slaves were literally worked to death. That was their fate also in Demerara, afterwards part of British Guiana, on the Success plantation, owned by the Gladstone family.[57] Throughout the West Indies slave mortality, especially infant mortality, was consistently high. In the mid-eighteenth century 5,000 slaves were dying each year in Barbados, out of a black population of 80,000.[58] Shortly before emancipation, British Guiana had a quaintly named 'Protector of Slaves', sent out from Britain. The holder of that office, a Captain Elliot, wrote in 1832: 'As to my office, it is a delusion. There is no protection for the Slave Population.' British Guiana's slaves endured punishments at a rate (in 1828) equivalent to one punishment for every third slave once a year. The colony's slave population declined by over 12 per cent between 1817 and 1833, and only a handful of that decline was accounted for by the freeing of slaves.[59]

The emerging industrial working class in Britain was exploited by the same capitalist class that exploited black slaves in the British West Indies, and was regarded by it in much the same light. When we ask, for instance, who it was that produced those textiles exported to Africa for the purchase of slaves, we find that a great many of the workers in the Lancashire mills were not adults, but the children of the urban poor. When the destitute parents were admitted to the parish workhouses, their children were taken from them and compulsorily bound apprentice to the cotton manufacturers. Factory children were first employed, at a Derby silk mill, in 1719; in 1767 Parliament gave permission for London poorhouse children to be apprenticed to textile mills; not until 1802 did legislation limit the working day of apprenticed children in the cotton and woollen mills to twelve hours. But this Act, the first piece of social legislation produced by the machine, remained a dead letter. When pauper apprentices fell asleep under the machines they were beaten back to work by overseers armed with billy-rollers or straps.[60] The cotton mills, crowded with overworked children, were hotbeds of typhus.[61] J. L. and Barbara Hammond, in a remarkable passage, traced the connection between this child serf system and the slave system that it directly served:

> An age that thought of the African negro, not as a person with a human life, but as so much labour power to be used in the service of a master or a system, came naturally to think of the poor at home in the same way ...
>
> The children of the poor were regarded as workers long before the Industrial Revolution. Locke suggested that they should begin work at three ... In the workhouses of large towns there was a quantity of child labour available for employment, that was even more powerless ... in the hands of a master than the stolen negro ... The new industry which was to give the English people such immense power in the world borrowed at its origin from the methods of the American settlements.
>
> When a London parish gave relief it generally claimed the right of disposing of all the children of the person receiving relief, and thus these London workhouses could be made to serve the purpose of the Lancashire cotton mills as the Guinea coast served that of the West Indian plantations. The analogy became painfully complete. In the

> *Assiento* the negroes are described as 'pieces', and the description would not be less suitable to the children taken for the mills.[62]

Sent to the north by wagon-loads at a time, the children were 'as much lost for ever to their parents as if they were shipped off to the West Indies'.[63] And one MP, addressing the Commons in 1811, used arguments in favour of this child serf system identical in substance with those used by the apologists of black slavery:

> Although in the higher ranks of society it was true that to cultivate the affections of children for their family was the source of every virtue, yet, that it was not so among the lower orders, and that it was a benefit to the children to take them away from their miserable and depraved parents ... It would be highly injurious to the public to put a stop to the binding so many apprentices to the cotton manufacturers, as it must necessarily raise the price of labour and enhance the price of cotton manufactured goods.[64]

3
India

Plunder

The East India Company, set up in 1600, was the first joint stock company of any importance. 'Joint stock' meant that members invested capital to be used jointly and received a share of the profits according to the size of their investment. It was the East India Company that founded British rule in India. But penetration of the sub-continent by these 'merchant adventurers' was at first very slow. Though they had a monopoly of the British share of the trade, they had to face stiff competition from Dutch, Portuguese, and French traders.

Three of the East India Company's ships visited the bustling city of Surat, 150 miles north of Bombay, in 1608, and four years later another of its ships dispersed a Portuguese squadron off Surat. After nearly three years' haggling, the local ruler gave the Company leave to build a 'factory', or permanent depot, at Surat in 1619. From this first base, the English were soon controlling the Arabian Sea and Persian Gulf. English imports of Gujarati calico 'pieces', 36ft to 45ft long, soared from 14,000 in 1619 to over 200,000 in 1625. In 1639 English merchants occupied what soon came to be called Madras, and within 20 years this had become the biggest 'factory' on India's east coast. In 1661 King Charles II of England obtained the island of Bombay from the Portuguese as part of the dowry of his bride, Catherine of Braganza. Easy to defend, Bombay was a highly convenient trading base; it was leased to the East India Company in 1668 for a rent of £10 a year, and the Company transferred its headquarters there in 1687. More than 100 English 'factors', or resident agents, were by now stationed in India. Having become 'a virtual state unto themselves', they were able to ensure an average annual profit for the Company of 25 per cent.[1]

The Company had its own private army, and in 1751 its defeat of a French puppet ruler put the Carnatic in English hands. This was a vast east-coast province stretching from well north of Madras right to the southern tip of India. Three years later the first British royal troops were landed; this was supposed to be a temporary measure, to ensure the defeat of the French. For a large area of India, the combination of

British royal troops and British 'merchant adventurers' proved disastrous.

In the 1750s the ruler (*nawab*) of Bengal was trying to get the British out before they got him out. An adventurer named Robert Clive defeated the *nawab*'s troops at the battle of Plassey (1757). This was the decisive turning-point, not only for British domination of India, but also for British extraction of wealth from India. From then on, mere trade would be supplemented by naked and rapacious plunder, backed by force of arms. Clive told the elder Pitt in 1759 that there would be 'little or no difficulty in obtaining the absolute possession of these rich kingdoms'.[2]

In the initial period, before they had the means to plunder India directly, British merchant capitalists had been forced to use some of the profits from elsewhere in the colonial system to pay for the goods they bought from the Indians. They coveted India's wealth, but at that stage they had to offer wealth in return. Once Britain had secured the *assiento* in 1713, they could offer silver bullion paid by Spain for those 4,800 African slaves the British were now under contract to supply each year. The slave trade and privateering gave them the necessary leverage. A European power with a surplus of silver 'had the advantage over all competitors'.[3] The British had that advantage, and they pressed it hard. 'The English trade with India', wrote the economic historian L. C. A. Knowles, 'was really a chase to find something that India would be willing to take, and the silver obtained by the sale of the slaves in the West Indies and Spanish America was all important in this connexion.'[4]

The battle of Plassey put an end once and for all to the need to send precious silver to India. Very soon there was widespread rejoicing that the British army's 'glorious successes' had

> brought near three millions of money to the nation; for ... almost the whole of the immense sums received ... finally centers in England. So great a proportion of it fell into the company's hands ... that they have been enabled to carry on the whole trade of India (China excepted) for three years together, without sending out one ounce of bullion.[5]

For the East India Company this was a dream come true. Now they could get their hands on India's wealth without having to send wealth in return. The first step was the assumption of the *dewani*, the right to collect the revenue in Bengal, Bihar and Orissa. There was traditionally in India an intimate relation between harvest and taxation. Before British rule there was no private property in land. The self-governing village community handed over each year to the ruler or his nominee the 'king's share' of the year's produce. The East India Company considered this practice barbarous, and put a stop to it. Under British rule a new revenue system was introduced, superseding the traditional right of the village community over land and creating two new forms of property in land: in some parts of the country, landlordism; in others, individual peasant proprietorship. It was assumed that the State was the supreme landlord, and there was introduced a system of fixed tax payments, assessed on land. Under the new system the cultivator had to pay a fixed sum to the government every year whether or not his crop had been successful. In years when the harvest was bad, the cultivators could only pay their taxes by recourse to moneylenders, whom the British authorities regarded as the mainstay for the payment of revenue and who frequently charged interest of 200 per cent annually or more. 'We introduced at one bound', a British writer later admitted, 'new methods of assessing and cultivating the land revenue, which have converted a once flourishing population into a huge horde of paupers.' Since peasants, in order to raise the cash demanded of them, were forced to sell their produce for whatever it would fetch, 'the first effect of British rule in an Indian province ... was ... to reduce the incomes of the agricultural classes by 50 per cent'.[6] The British conquest undermined the agrarian economy and the self-governing village.

The assumption of the *dewani* gave the East India Company not only the entire revenue of the eastern provinces but also enormous political and economic power. This power was soon used to get rid of French, Dutch, and Danish 'factories'; to prevent Indian and other merchants from trading in grain, salt, betel nuts, and tobacco; and to discourage handicrafts. In 1769 the Company prohibited the home work of the silk weavers and compelled them to work in its factories.[7] The Company's servants, who lined their pockets by private trading, bribery and extortion, arbitrarily decided how much cloth each weaver should deliver and how much he should receive for it. Weavers who disobeyed were seized, imprisoned, fined or flogged. Weavers unable to meet the obligations the Company imposed on them had their possessions confiscated and sold on the spot. Bengal's ruler complained that the Company's agents were taking away people's goods by force for a quarter of their value and compelling people to buy from them at five times the value of the goods bought, on pain of a flogging or imprisonment.[8] By the 1770s Bengal had become 'one continued scene of oppression'.[9] Systematic plunder led to a famine in which 10 million people perished: 'Bengal was left naked, stripped of its surplus wealth and grain. In the wake of British spoliation, famine struck and in 1770 alone took the lives of an estimated one-third of Bengal's peasantry.'[10] A Commons Select Committee reported in 1783 that 'the Natives of all Ranks and Orders' had been reduced to a 'State of Depression and Misery'.[11] Four years later a former army officer, William Fullarton, wrote:

> In former times the Bengal countries were the granary of nations, and the repository of commerce, wealth and manufacture in the East ... But such has been the restless energy of our misgovernment, that within the short space of twenty years many parts of those countries have been reduced to the appearance of a desert. The fields are no longer cultivated, – extensive tracts are already overgrown with thickets, – the husbandman is plundered, – the manufacturer oppressed, – famine has been repeatedly endured, – and depopulation has ensued.[12]

A chancellor of the exchequer frankly told the Commons in 1858 that 'no civilized Government ever existed on the face of this earth which was more corrupt, more perfidious, and more rapacious than the Government of the East India Company from the years 1765 to 1784'.[13] This rapacity brought treasure flowing into Britain 'in oceans'.[14] As India became poor and hungry, Britain became richer than ever before. Clive, penniless when he first landed in India, sent back to Britain nearly a third of the revenue he collected, and went back home with a personal fortune estimated at £250,000. It was in this period that the Hindi word 'loot' entered the English language; and it has been estimated that, between the battle of Plassey in 1757 and the battle of Waterloo in 1815, Britain's loot from India was worth between £500 million and £1,000 million.[15]

This loot from India furnished the second of those 'special forced draughts' which were needed to ignite Britain's industrial revolution. Close on the heels of the battle of Plassey came the harnessing, in rapid succession, of a critical series of inventions and technological advances. Hargreaves's spinning jenny (1764), Arkwright's water-frame (1769), and Crompton's mule (1779) broke with the old hand techniques. In 1785 came the next logical step: the adaptation of Watt's steam engine to drive them. The increase in productivity was explosive. Between 1767 and 1787 the output of cotton goods went up more than fivefold.[16]

But Britain's enrichment at the expense of the Indian people had only begun. In the nineteenth century it was to take new and, in many ways, still more oppressive forms.

De-industrialization

When European merchant adventurers first reached India they did not find an industrial or technical backwater. On the contrary, 'the industrial development of the country was at any rate not inferior to that of the more advanced European nations.'[17] India was not only a great agricultural country but also a great manufacturing country. It had a prosperous textile industry,whose cotton, silk, and woollen products were marketed in Europe as well as elsewhere in Asia. It had remarkable, and remarkably ancient, skills in iron-working. It had its own shipbuilding industry: Calcutta, Daman, Surat, Bombay, and Pegu were important shipbuilding centres, and in 1802 skilled Indian workers were building British warships at the Bombay shipyard of Bomenjee and Manseckjee. It was generally acknowledged that 'the teak-wood vessels of Bombay were greatly superior to the oaken walls of Old England'.[18] Benares was famous all over India for its brass, copper and bell-metal wares. Other important industries included the enamelled jewellery and stone-carving of the Rajputana towns, as well as filigree work in gold and silver, ivory, glass, tannery, perfumery and paper-making.[19]

All this was altered under British rule. The long-term consequence of that rule was the de-industrialization of India – its forcible transformation from a country of combined agriculture and manufacture into an agricultural colony of British capitalism, exporting to Britain raw cotton, wool, jute, oilseeds, dyes and hides.[20] The British annihilated the Indian textile industry 'with the fury of a forest fire'; a dangerous competitor existed, and it had to be destroyed.[21] The shipbuilding industry aroused the jealousy of British firms, 'and its progress and development were restricted by legislation'.[22] India's metalwork, glass and paper industries were likewise throttled, the latter being deprived of its greatest patron when an order of Sir Charles Wood, Secretary of State for India, 1859–66, obliged the British government in India to use only British-made paper. The vacuum created by the contrived ruin of the Indian handicraft industries, a process virtually completed by 1880, was filled with British manufactured goods.

Britain's industrial revolution, with its explosive increase in productivity, made it essential for British capitalists to find new markets. So in India the previous monopoly had to give way to a free market. From an exporter of textiles, India had to become an importer of textiles. British goods had to have virtually free entry, while the entry into Britain of Indian manufactured goods, especially silks and cottons, had to be blocked by prohibitive tariffs. And direct trade between India and the rest of the world had to be curtailed. By 1840 British silk and cotton goods imported into India paid a duty of only three-and-a-half per cent, woollen goods a mere two per cent. Equivalent Indian exports to Britain paid import duties of 20, 10, and 30 per cent respectively.[23]

> Had not such prohibitory duties and decrees existed, the mills of Paisley and of Manchester would have been stopped ... They were created by the sacrifice of the Indian manufacture ... The foreign manufacturer employed the arm of political injustice to keep down and ultimately strangle a competitor with whom he could not have contended on equal terms.[24]

So there was prosperity for the British cotton industry and ruin for millions of Indian craftsmen and artisans. India's rich manufacturing towns were blighted: towns like Surat, where it had all begun 200 years before; Decca, once known as 'the Manchester of India'; Murshidabad, Bengal's old capital, said in 1757 to be as extensive, populous and rich as London. Millions of spinners and weavers were forced to seek a precarious living in the countryside, as were many tanners, smelters, and smiths. The development of Indian cotton mills in the 1870s, coupled with a trade slump in Britain, led Lancashire textile manufacturers to press for total repeal of Indian cotton duties, which had given some small protection to the Indian cotton industry as well as 'retaining labour in the industrial sector which could more usefully be employed in growing cotton for export to Lancashire'.[25] The Lancashire capitalists had their way. In 1879 Viceroy Lytton 'overruled his entire council to accommodate Lancashire's lobby by removing all import duties on British-made cotton, despite India's desperate need for more revenue in a year of widespread famine'.[26] In the last 20 years of the nineteenth century India's own production of cloth met less than 10 per cent of home demand, while Lancashire products accounted for between one-half and two-thirds of India's annual imports.

Britain, whose queen had been proclaimed Empress of India in 1876, had made India subservient to British industry and its needs and was continuing to suck vast wealth out of the sub-continent. Generations of Indian economists and nationalist politicians, supported by a small number of British opponents of colonialism, complained of this drain of wealth, analysed its mechanisms in copious detail, proved their case with massive evidence from official sources, and showed how this economic exploitation was the root cause of the Indian people's poverty and hunger.[27]

From time to time officialdom was forced to curb the worst excesses. One example of this is the inquiry into the plantation system for cultivating indigo. That system began in 1833, when English people were first allowed to acquire land in India and set up as planters there. Significantly, 1833 was also the year when the law was passed to free Britain's black slaves in the Caribbean. And many of those who started growing indigo in the deltaic area of lower Bengal were experienced sugar planters from the Caribbean. As one economic historian puts it, 'the area attracted a rather rough set of planters, some of whom had been slave drivers in America and carried unfortunate ideas and practices with them'.[28] Following the so-called 'Blue Mutiny' of 1859–60 – in effect the first strike by Indians against British management (see p. 111 below) – an official inquiry brought to light monstrous abuses by the British planters and their Indian assistants. The Indigo Commission's report showed that the plantation system in Bengal was slavery under another name. *Ryots* (peasants) who objected to sowing indigo were murdered; their houses were pulled down; they were kidnapped and locked up; their cattle were seized; their very gardens were grubbed up to make room for indigo.[29] A hundred years later the word 'indigo', to Indians, still stood for British 'greed, dishonesty and oppression ... Unquestionably this is one of the dark episodes in the history of British dealings with a subject people.'[30]

But though specific abuses were checked from time to time, abuse continued. Under British imperial rule the ordinary people of India grew steadily poorer. At the start of the twentieth century the economic historian Romesh Dutt called Indian poverty 'unparalleled'. Half of India's annual net revenues of £44 million, he calculated, flowed out of India.[31] The number of famines soared from 7 in the first half of the nineteenth century to 24 in the second half. According to official figures, 28,825,000 Indians starved to death between 1854 and 1901.[32] The terrible famine of 1899–1900, which affected 475,000 square miles with a population of almost 60 million, was attributed to a process of bleeding the peasants, who were forced into the clutches of moneylenders whom the British authorities regarded as their mainstay for the payment of revenue.[33] The Bengal famine of 1943, which claimed 1,500,000 victims, was accentuated by the authorities' carelessness and utter lack of foresight, and the Famine Inquiry Commission severely criticized the 'administrative breakdown'.[34] Only a high death rate – in Bombay it was 667 per 1,000 in 1921 – prevented still worse famines.

Rich though its soil was, India's people were hungry, and miserably poor. This grinding poverty 'struck all visitors ... like a blow in the face'.[35] That was how it struck the delegation which visited India on behalf of the India League in 1932. The delegation – one of whose members, Ellen Wilkinson, was later to be Minister of Education in the 1945 Labour government – spent 83 days in India, meeting Indians of every class and shade of opinion. In their report, *Condition of India* (1934), they said they had been

> appalled at the poverty of the Indian village. It is the home of stark want ... From province to province conditions vary, but the results of uneconomic agriculture, peasant indebtedness, excessive taxation and rack-renting, absence of social services and the general discontent impressed us everywhere ... In the villages we saw, there were no health or sanitary services, there were no roads, no drainage or lighting, and no proper water supply beyond the village well ...
>
> Men, women and children work in the fields, farms and cowsheds ... All alike work on meagre food and comfort and toil long hours for inadequate returns.[36]

In short, throughout the British occupation, millions of Indians could never get enough food, and at least two-thirds of the people connected, directly or indirectly, with agriculture lived 'in a state of squalor'.[37] On the eve of the British withdrawal in 1947, Jawaharlal Nehru wrote that those parts of India which had been longest under British rule were the poorest: 'Bengal, once so rich and flourishing, after 187 years of British rule ... is ... a miserable mass of poverty-stricken, starving, and dying people'.[38]

To maintain their economic exploitation of India the British had imposed a despotic system of political control. That system was locked in place in 1858 in direct response to the Indian people's first national uprising, the so-called 'Mutiny' of 1857–8 (see pp. 108–11). This mass uprising was suppressed at a cost of £36 million, a full year's worth of Indian revenues. To consolidate their expensively regained mastery of the sub-continent, the British government took direct control. All the rights the East India Company had hitherto enjoyed on Indian soil were transferred to the Crown. Thus was inaugurated 'an era of complete despotism such as the Mughals themselves might have envied'.[39] After 78 years of direct rule, Britain still governed India by naked coercion: the police mentality pervaded all spheres of government, and a vast army of spies and secret agents covered the land. The British in India felt and behaved like members of an army of occupation. And the outstanding feature of British rule was their concentration on everything that served to strengthen their political and economic grip.[40]

4
The Caribbean from 1834

The Abolition of Slavery

Slavery was legally ended throughout the British Empire on 1 August 1834. As a system of production, it was becoming increasingly unprofitable. There was a strong abolitionist movement in Britain, where the demand for abolition was not confined to middle-class humanitarians but was central to the radical working-class movement. International and intercolonial rivalries also played a large part in bringing about abolition. Above all, the Caribbean was seething with unrest. A black revolution throughout the British West Indies, designed to abolish slavery from below, was 'widely apprehended, both in the West Indies and in Britain'.[1] And it was in fact the Jamaican uprising of 1831–32, the so-called 'Baptist War' (see pp. 92–5 below), 'that proved the decisive factor precipitating emancipation'.[2]

But Britain's 540,559 black slaves in the Caribbean – whose owners were compensated for their lost property to the tune of a staggering £20 million – did not become free overnight. The legislation that ended slavery imposed a period of what was called 'apprenticeship'. The former slaves stayed tied to the soil of the sugar plantations for a further four years, during which they were obliged to perform 45 hours of *unpaid* labour per week for their former masters.

The planters feared that emancipation would bring about their ruin. They were scared that the ex-slaves would not want to go on producing sugar for them, even for wages. In Barbados it was suggested that the ex-slaves' provision grounds should be grubbed up, to force them to work. In British Guiana the planters cut down fruit trees, destroyed plantain walks, and banned fishing, so that freed slaves should be denied any source of food that might compete with plantation work.[3] The planters' fears were not groundless. There was indeed an exodus from the plantations. Ex-slaves turned to three alternative sources of livelihood: small-scale local trading; skilled trades; and subsistence farming.[4] By 1840 women and children in Jamaica were refusing to work on the plantations; men were working irregularly and often negligently; and thousands of ex-slaves were settling in vacant backlands. Six years later the labouring population residing on the estates was only a third of what it had been in the last years of slavery.[5] In Trinidad and British Guiana, too, freed slaves streamed off the estates, despite the planters' promises of free housing, high wages, and numerous allowances.[6] The planters had only one effective remedy: to recruit a fresh labour force, cheap and easily disciplined. Their eyes turned greedily to India.

Indentured Labour

The large-scale importation of free workers from India was first proposed in 1814 by a leading Trinidad planter who soon won the support of the colony's governor. The Gladstone family, which received the largest sum paid out in compensation – £85,606 0*s.* 2*d.* for 2,183 slaves set free in British Guiana and Jamaica – enthusiastically sponsored the idea. Immigration from India began in 1838, was halted for several years, resumed, and halted again. British Guiana and Trinidad began to take immigrants once more in 1851 and Jamaica followed suit seven years later. The system lasted until 1917. During those eight decades approximately 500,000 poor Indians left the poverty and hunger of British India and endured a nightmare voyage of three or four months, in the hope of building a better life for themselves in the British West Indies. About 238,000 went to British Guiana, 145,000 to Trinidad and 21,500 to Jamaica.

In folk art the indentured Indian was always depicted hunched up, hands tied together; and the indentured labour system was indeed a kind of serfdom. Recruited by agents at Calcutta and Madras, who toured villages where the crops had failed and told of easy work for high wages, the Indians signed contracts, the men generally for five years, the women for three. The laws were heavily weighted against them. They were held criminally liable for even the most trivial breaches of contract. Absence from work for seven consecutive days was regarded as desertion and was punishable, in British Guiana, by a fine of 24 dollars or one month's imprisonment with hard labour. In Trinidad the maximum penalty for this crime was two months' imprisonment, while for using threatening language to an overseer, for negligence, or for hindering or molesting other immigrants in their work, an indentured labourer could be fined £5 or jailed for two months. Though most left India totally ignorant of the conditions under which they would have to work, the immigrants had no freedom whatever to withdraw from the contract. Nor could they move from one estate to another – nor, indeed, leave their own estate without a pass (*livret*) describing the place and nature of their work. In most of the sugar colonies Indians still had to carry a pass after their indenture period was completed. In British Guiana an immigrant found without a pass two miles away from his estate was liable to arrest without a warrant by a police officer or rural constable. The system was carefully designed to immobilize labour, to anchor immigrants on each estate so that labour might be always conveniently at hand.

Runaways, and sick men suspected of malingering, were flogged with cat-o'-nine-tails, twisted ropes, or rattan canes. Workers were also flogged for lateness, insolence, and refusing to obey an order. Right into the twentieth century beatings and floggings were a matter of routine. In British Guiana, until the 1870s, planters also used the stocks as a punishment. The colonial authorities were assured that the punishments imposed would not, in India, be declared an abuse. The immigrants were housed in barracks that were often scarcely better than mule-pens. They were not given enough to eat, were paid a pittance, and when they fell sick were not properly cared for. All this led to an appalling death rate in the system's earlier years. Of the 11,434 Indians who landed in British Guiana between 1845 and 1849, no fewer than 2,218 had died on the estates, in jails, or in hospitals by the end of 1849, while another 2,159 were 'unaccounted for'. It was said that immigrants' bones were strewn on the streets.[7] In Trinidad 'the decaying remains of immigrants were frequently discovered in cane fields and woodlands throughout the colony'.[8] In Jamaica and Grenada, too, Indians who fell sick were turned off the estates and left to die on the roads.[9] In later years, throughout the British West Indies, mortality varied roughly between 2 per cent and 4 per cent of the indentured population each year.[10] Most of the Indian immigrants died without issue: 'only a tiny minority ... had children to claim their share in the lands where the pioneers struggled and died'.[11]

The labour of these indentured Indians saved the sugar economy in Trinidad and British Guiana and made a major contribution to Britain's overseas wealth. This profitable 'coolie' system was built on the foundations laid by the slave system it so closely resembled. Overseers who prided themselves as disciplinarians claimed to have their indentured immigrants 'always either at work, or in hospital, or in gaol'.[12] The practice of successive reindentures, tempting with large bounties those who had worked out their time, condemned most of the immigrants to perpetual indenture. In Hugh Tinker's words, indenture

> did, indeed, replicate the actual conditions of slavery ... For a period of seventy or eighty years British statesmen and administrators were

> being confronted with evidence that the planting interest was exploiting Indian workers in ways which could not be tolerated by a decent, humane society: and yet they continued to assure themselves that these wrongs were mere abuses and irregularities which could be amenable to reform.[13]

In the end, the system was done away with only as the result of an outcry from Indian public opinion – to which the British authorities thought it wise to make such a concession at a time when the nationalist movement was gaining strength.[14] (For Indian indentured labour elsewhere in the British Empire, see pp. 47–8.)

Apprenticeship

In the years of apprenticeship (1834–38) the former slaves in the British West Indies were hemmed in by a comprehensive system of restriction in the shape of Trespass Acts and Vagrant Acts.[15] People found guilty under this legislation did not serve their sentences in the jails, which were generally reserved for white criminals, but in workhouses or houses of correction. Here the warders were long-term convicts. It was normal for the prisoners to be taken out of the workhouses to work in chains and iron collars, and the appearance of such penal gangs in the streets of Kingston and Spanish Town – including mothers suckling babies – startled visitors who supposed that such sights had vanished with slavery.[16] The imprisoned apprentices, consigned to the workhouse for totally trivial offences, endured solitary confinement in dark cells on a starvation diet. Females were raped by the convict-drivers. Prisoners were often flogged and some were flogged to death. Frederick Shrieves, an old man suffering from elephantiasis, was flogged to death in the Hanover workhouse, and the three who stood trial for his murder were found not guilty. Another apprentice, Anna Maria Thompson, was flogged to death in the Buff Bay workhouse. Ailing men and pregnant women alike were, in these workhouses, tortured on treadmills designed to mash their legs and sickeningly stained with their blood, and these atrocities continued even after magistrates had explicitly forbidden such treatment. In the St Thomas-in-the-East workhouse alone, eleven apprentices died in twelve months as a result of the treadmill. 'It is ... proper', comments W. L. Burn, 'that we see what happened to the Jamaica negro in the workhouse, since it was part of the boon of emancipation which Parliament had conferred on him.'[17]

Britain's 'Tropical Farms'

When apprenticeship came to an end in 1838, two years earlier than at first intended, Britain had control of Jamaica, Barbados, Trinidad, Tobago, the Leeward and Windward Islands, the Bahamas, the Turks and Caicos Islands, British Honduras and British Guiana. In Barbados all available land was occupied; but in several of the other colonies an independent peasantry came into being, by a remarkable process of self-help and solidarity that was not at all to the taste of the planters, who did their best to put a stop to it.

The movement was most powerful in British Guiana, where, despite a decision that land should not be sold to emancipated slaves, many pooled their resources to buy up abandoned estates. First to do so were 83 ex-slaves, five of them women, who in 1839 bought a 500-acre cotton plantation for $10,000 – 'a remarkable tribute to their thrift during apprenticeship'.[18] There is a tradition that they took the money to the vendors in wheelbarrows, in coins of small denomination. By 1850, of a total Afro-Guyanese labouring population of 82,000, over 42,000 had succeeded in making themselves at least partly independent of plantation work. They had established 25 communal villages at an aggregate cost (dwellings included) of almost $2,250,000, 'a staggering achievement for a people just twelve years out of slavery'.[19] But the authorities stepped in. On the one hand, they limited the number of joint purchasers, first to 20 (in 1852), then to 10 (in 1856). On the other, they refused to give help, notably for sea-defence and drainage. The planters controlled the legislature, and their main aim was command of the labour market. They did not want the peasants' settlements to succeed. And, as the planters intended, poverty forced many back into partial dependence on the plantations as a source of livelihood.

Similar settlements, following the end of apprenticeship, sprang up in Jamaica and Trinidad. In Jamaica, by 1843, some 19,000 ex-slaves had bought land and were building their own cottages. But in Trinidad estate managers and government collaborated to make land prices too high for most would-be settlers.

The overwhelming majority of the populations of these colonies, whether of African or Asian descent, had no say whatever in the making of decisions that affected their lives. Representative government was out of the question, as that would have meant giving black people the vote. And this was something the British were not prepared to do. They said so quite openly. The Duke of Newcastle, soon to become Colonial Secretary, told the House of Lords in 1858 that responsible government for the colonies was 'only applicable to colonists of the English race'.[20] And in 1884 a Royal Commission appointed to inquire into the public revenues, expenditure, debts, and liabilities of Jamaica, Grenada and other islands, took the same view: 'as the employers and employed will be generally speaking of different races, the Imperial Government will continue to have an ultimate responsibility in the administration of these islands, and must consequently retain an adequate proportion of direct power in the administration.' After all, the Caribbean islands were 'the tropical farms of the English nation', said this Royal Commission of 100 years ago.[21]

The beasts of burden in these tropical farms were black people. Another Royal Commission, in 1897, admitted that 'we have placed the labouring population where it is, and created for it the conditions ... under which it exists' – those conditions being 'distress' and difficulty in finding a livelihood.[22] After three centuries of British rule the tropical farms' main crops were extreme poverty, hardship, disease, illiteracy, and slum housing. In the 1930s, wrote Eric Williams,

> the Barbadian labourer was fed worse than a gaolbird; he could not afford milk in his tea; said the planters, he did not like milk! ...
>
> The daily consumption of fresh milk in Kingston, Jamaica, with its 30,000 children of school age, was one-fifteenth of a quart per head; the Jamaican politicians in the age of colonialism said the Negroes preferred condensed milk ...
>
> An official picture of Trinidad in 1937 described every adult over twenty years of age as affected by deficiency diseases, and the working life of the population reduced by at least one-half ...
>
> What, then, of the children? With the mother debilitated by hookworm, half-starved and vulnerable to waterborne diseases, the infant mortality rate was staggering. For Trinidad it was 120 per 1,000 live births; for Jamaica 137; for Antigua 171; for St Kitts 187; for Barbados 217; as compared with 58 in England ...
>
> Of the total deaths in Jamaica in 1935, over 33 per cent were of infants under five years of age. An examination of 12,000 schoolchildren in Kingston revealed that 40 per cent were undernourished.[23]

In 1938-39 yet another Royal Commission, chaired by Lord Moyne, investigated social conditions in Barbados, British Guiana, British Honduras, Jamaica, the Leeward Islands, Trinidad and Tobago, and the Windward Islands. The Moyne Commission submitted its report at the end of 1939, but it was such a revealing document that the British government thought it had better not be published until the Second World War was over, and it did not appear until June 1945. It painted a grim picture of the British Empire's neglected backwater.

In some parts of the British West Indies, said the Moyne Commission's report, rates for agricultural labourers had advanced little beyond the shilling-a-day introduced after emancipation. The rate was 1*s*. 2*d*. a day in St Kitts, 1*s*. 3*d*. (1*s*. 0*d*. for women) in Grenada and St Lucia, 1*s*. 1*d*. (10*d*. for women) in St Vincent, 2*s*. 2*d*. (1*s*. 6 1/2*d*. for women) in British Guiana, 1*s*. 10*d*. (1*s*. 0*d*. for women) in Trinidad, and 1*s*. 10*d*. in Jamaica. Matters were scarcely better in the towns: 'The condition of many of the townspeople, as we saw for ourselves, is pitiable.' On education, the Moyne Commission had this to say:

> An examination of the working of the educational system ... reveals serious inadequacies in almost every respect. There is not nearly enough accommodation for the children who attend schools; and these include by no means all the children of school age. Existing accommodation is frequently ... in a chronic state of disrepair and insanitation. Teachers are inadequate in number, and are in most Colonies not well paid. Their training is largely defective or non-existent.

On health and housing, the Moyne Commission reported that 'chronic sickness among the people of the West Indian Colonies is common', and it went on to show why:

> In both town and country the present housing of the large majority of the working people in the West Indian Colonies leaves much to be desired; in many places it is deplorable; in some the conditions are such that any human habitation of buildings now occupied by large families must seem impossible to a newcomer from Europe. It is no exaggeration to say that in the poorest parts of most towns and in many of the country districts a majority of the houses is largely made of rusty corrugated iron and unsound boarding; quite often the original floor has disappeared and only the earth remains ... sanitation in any form and water supply are unknown in such premises, and in many cases no light can enter when the door is closed. These decrepit houses, more often than not, are seriously overcrowded, and it is not surprising that some of them are dirty and verminous in spite of the praiseworthy efforts of the inhabitants to keep them clean. In short, every condition that tends to produce disease is here to be found in a serious form. The generally insanitary environment gives rise to

> malaria, worm infection and bowel diseases; leaking roofs, rotten flooring, and lack of light encourage the spread of tuberculosis, respiratory diseases, worm infections, jigger-lesions and rat-borne diseases; overcrowding, which is usually accompanied by imperfect ventilation, is an important agent in contributing to the high incidence of yaws, tuberculosis, venereal diseases and, to a certain extent, leprosy.[24]

It was to get away from such conditions – in essence unchanged in the ten years since the Moyne Commission's visit – and to try to build a new and more tolerable life for themselves that black people from the Caribbean began settling in Britain in 1948.

5
Africa (Other Than Southern Africa)

Just as British capitalism distorted India's economy in order to obtain the highest possible amount of wealth, so Britain, in common with other European powers, distorted Africa's economy for the same purpose. This distortion began long before the era of colonial rule. By the time Africa entered the colonial era its unequal trading relationship with Europe had already led to the stagnation of African technology. In particular, European traders had destroyed the African cloth industry based on handlooms and small-scale craft production. They had done so partly by controlling the distribution of cloth around the African coast, and partly by swamping African products with bulk imports of manufactured cloth. By the nineteenth century, Africa was exporting raw cotton and importing manufactured cotton cloth. The only technology that European capitalism was willing to transfer to Africa was firearms. Requests for other skills and techniques were ignored or rejected.[1]

After four centuries of unequal trade the stage was eventually reached where it was both possible and necessary to combine 'developed' Europe and 'underdeveloped' Africa in a single colonialist system. By the last quarter of the nineteenth century European capitalism had three supreme needs: new sources of raw materials; new markets for manufactured goods; and new profitable fields of investment. These needs were met by what was soon acknowledged to be a scramble for African territory.

Africa's greatest value to European capitalism lay in its ability to satisfy the first of these needs: raw materials. Above all, European industry needed African cotton, rubber and palm oil. Until about 1875 this need could be satisfied by carving Africa up into informal spheres of influence. But the time came when gentlemen's agreements about trading areas were no longer enough. They had to be replaced by naked colonial domination. The scramble for Africa – the conquest of almost the entire continent by the European powers – was already under way when it was decided to bring about a certain measure of coordination. At the 1884–85 Berlin Conference, Britain, Germany, Belgium, France, Italy, Portugal and several other powers met to dovetail their plans for completing the territorial division of Africa. They were careful to hide their true purpose under a high-flown avowal of moral aims. After Berlin the scramble for Africa was pursued with vigour, greed and devastating fire-power. The Maxim gun, a lethal machine-gun, was invented at the very time of the Berlin Conference. Here was one kind of gun the British were not prepared to export to Africans. In Hilaire Belloc's words,

> Whatever happens we have got
> The Maxim Gun, and they have not.[2]

With the help of such murderous weapons, more than 10 million square miles of African territory and over 100 million Africans were brought under European rule in hardly more than a decade.[3] With considerable satisfaction, the geographer Sir John Scott Keltie observed in 1893: 'We have been witnesses of one of the most remarkable episodes in the history of the world. During the past eight years we have seen the bulk of the one barbarous continent parcelled out among the most civilised Powers of Europe.'[4]

Britain had long held a number of coastal strips in West Africa: the Gambia, where Britain had possessed a base since 1662 and where a British settlement was established in 1816; Sierra Leone, which became a British colony in 1807; Lagos, occupied in 1861; and the southern Gold Coast, annexed in 1874. In southern Africa, the Cape of Good Hope had been occupied since 1806 and Natal since 1843; and Basutoland had been annexed in 1868. Following the Berlin Conference, the British lost no time in mopping up all they could of the territories that remained. Bechuanaland was made a 'protectorate' in 1885. The occupation of Nigeria was formally complete by 1886, though much of the country stayed independent for several more years. Somaliland was occupied in 1886; Zululand was annexed in 1887; then Kenya the following year. Rhodesia came under British rule in 1888–93, Zanzibar in 1890, Uganda in 1890–96 and Nyasaland in 1891. Ashanti was conquered in 1901 and the British colony of the Gold Coast was established in 1902. The British 'sphere of influence' also included Egypt, occupied in 1882 and declared independent in 1922, and the oddly named Anglo-Egyptian Sudan, where British control was established in 1899 in the guise of a joint administration. In the scramble for Africa, the British lion had succeeded in grabbing the lion's share. British capital, and the international banking groups associated with it, also dominated the Portuguese African colonies of Angola, Mozambique and Portuguese Guinea; and British interests had a substantial share in the exploitation of the Belgian Congo.

Following the First World War (1914–18), which was above all a war for the redistribution of the loot, Britain received a League of Nations mandate to administer some of the former German colonies in Africa. Britain and Belgium divided the former German East Africa between them, the British share being called Tanganyika Territory. Britain and France sliced up Kamerun and Togo. German South-West Africa went to the Union of South Africa.

All these vast acquisitions of African territory were directly controlled by various capitalist groups and companies, such as the United Africa Company, a subsidiary of Unilever. These concerns were able to reap huge profits, especially from the mining of gold, diamonds, manganese, copper, iron ore, bauxite and tin. The Africans who worked for these European companies were ruthlessly exploited. Between the First and Second World Wars, Nigerian coalminers at Enugu earned a shilling a day for underground work, ninepence a day for surface work.[5] In 1937 Nigerian tin-miners took home, on average, 3*s*. 6*d*. a week, and the industry's total annual wage bill of £329,000 was hardly more than a quarter of its total profit of £1,249,000.[6] In Northern Rhodesia's copper mines, developed in the late 1920s by the Rhodesian Selection Trust and the Anglo-American Corporation, unskilled labourers earned as little as 7*s*. a month. White truck drivers on the copper belt were paid £30 a month, black truck drivers £3 a month.[7] Northern Rhodesia's output of copper in 1937 – all sold outside the colony – was worth about £12 million. Of the proceeds, about £5 million went in dividends to non-resident shareholders, and £500,000 was paid in royalties to the British South Africa Company, which owned all the colony's minerals by virtue of a treaty made 40 years before with the king of the Barotse. The wage bill for the 17,000 black workers totalled £244,000, an average of 5*s*. 6*d*. per head per week.[8] In 1934, when 41 Africans were killed in a Gold Coast gold-mine disaster, the employers offered £3 to each worker's dependants as compensation. British capitalist rule in Africa was truly 'exploitation without responsibility and without redress'.[9]

In many areas Africans were robbed wholesale of their best land. In Kenya's Njoro district, for instance, Lord Delamere acquired 100,000 acres of the best land in 1903 at the cost of one penny per acre. Adjoining his estate, Lord Francis Scott took 350,000 acres of this 'Crown Land', East African Estates Ltd took 350,000 acres, and the East African Syndicate took 100,000 acres, all dirt-cheap.[10] Dispossessed Africans were relegated to reserves and obliged to endure various forms of economic coercion, notably the compulsory cultivation of certain crops and forced labour for 'public works' – i.e. 'building castles for governors, prisons for Africans, barracks for troops, and bungalows for colonial officials' as well as 'roads, railways and ports to provide the infrastructure for private capitalist investment and to facilitate the export of cash crops'.[11] These peasant cash crops were bought at well under world market prices. Thus in 1946 the West African Produce Control Board paid Nigerians just under £17 for a ton of palm oil which they sold through the British Ministry of Food for £95.[12]

The colonial domination of Africa was an integral system whose central purpose was the transfer of a massive surplus from Africa to European capitalism, which was thereby given a new lease of life. This system's overall effect on Africa was to distort still further the continent's economy, to continue and intensify the underdevelopment that had resulted from the unequal trading relations of the pre-colonial era. In particular, colonial domination prevented the industrialization of Africa. To the traveller Mary Kingsley, writing in 1897, West Africa would 'for hundreds of years' supply the European manufacturer with his raw materials and take his manufactured articles in exchange, 'giving him a good margin of profit'.[13] And indeed, 'by the end of the colonial era, the African continent as a whole remained economically backward ... Africa was developed, above all, to supply export crops and raw materials to meet the needs of Europe'.[14] Kwame Nkrumah wrote of pre-independence Ghana:

> Under colonial rule, foreign monopoly interests had our whole economy tied up to suit themselves. In a country whose output of cocoa is the largest in the world, there was not a single chocolate factory. While we produce the raw materials for the manufacture of soap and edible fats, palm products, the manufacture of these items was discouraged. A British firm owning lime plantations here ... actually expresses the juice from the fruit before shipping it in bulk to the United Kingdom and exporting it back to us, bottled, to retail in stores at a high price ... These facts have a kind of Alice in Wonderland craziness about them ... They are implicit in the whole concept and policy of colonialism.
>
> It is estimated that during the last thirty years of British colonial administration, British trading and shipping interests took out of our country a total of £300,000,000. Just imagine what might have been done by way of development if only part of these gigantic transfers of profit had been retained and used for the benefit of our people ...
>
> Under the British there was no poultry farming to speak of; there was no proper dairy farming, and the ordinary Gold Coast family never saw a glass of fresh milk in its life. There was no raising of beef

> cattle. There were no industrial crops ...
>
> However wise, enlightened and good-hearted certain individual officers may have been, their functions and authority fitted into a pattern of colonial administration which was itself conditioned by the central and over-all need to extract the riches of the colonies and transfer them overseas.[15]

From Ghana – Britain's 'Gold Coast' – we turn lastly to Nigeria, Britain's largest colony, for an official report on social conditions towards the end of British rule. The House of Commons Select Committee on Estimates reported in 1948 that Nigeria had one doctor for every 133,000 people compared with one for every 1,200 people in the United Kingdom. It had one hospital bed for every 3,700 people compared with one for every 250 people in the UK. There were 10 dentists. Over 20 million people (in a population variously estimated at 22 million and 25 million) were living by very low-order subsistence agriculture. Malnutrition and disease were widespread. No health statistics were available, but in Lagos, the capital, infant mortality was stated to be 110 compared with 40 to 50 in Europe. Tuberculosis accounted for an estimated 9 to 10 per cent of all deaths, yet the colony had not a single sanatorium; the disease was treated in ordinary hospitals. At all hospitals there were long waiting lists and, in some, patients had to be put on the floor. Out of about 8 million children under the age of 16, over 7,300,000 were receiving no education at all, and such technical education as existed was 'totally inadequate'.[16]

Such was the legacy of underdevelopment that Britain bequeathed to its colonies in black Africa.

6
Territories of White Settlement

The British Empire included a number of territories – Tasmania, Australia, New Zealand and South Africa – where white people settled as convicts or farmers. These settlers appropriated the land of the original inhabitants, who were customarily treated with great inhumanity.

Tasmania

Tasmania was the home of hunter-gatherers who had lived in isolation from the rest of humankind for 8,000–10,000 years, perhaps considerably longer. The first Europeans to arrive, in 1772, found them hospitable; their ethical code attached much importance to sharing and giving. Before long, many of the estimated 4,000 black Tasmanians had been infected with diseases brought by their visitors. Then the outcasts of the British social system were set loose to take the Tasmanians' land, so causing them a serious food shortage. For 30 years black Tasmanians were pitilessly hunted down, tortured and put to death. Men and boys were castrated and otherwise mutilated; women were raped, flogged and burnt with brands; children's brains were dashed out. Some black Tasmanians were tied to trees and used as targets for shooting practice. One old woman was roasted alive. Another woman had her dead husband's head hung round her neck and was driven in front of her captor as his prize. One settler kept a pickle-tub into which he tossed the ears of the black people he shot.

In 1831 the 203 survivors of these atrocities were transported to Flinders Island in the Furneaux Group, which became a sort of human zoo-cum-cemetery. Each morning at sunrise they would climb a hill to gaze across the water at the mountains of Tasmania and, raising their arms, would cry with tears streaming down their faces: 'Country belonging to me.'[1] After 15 years about 40 were still alive, and these were taken back to the mainland and housed in an old convict barracks. They knew they had been brought back to die and, one by one, they died of despair. Within 75 years of the first British settlement in 1803,

Tasmania's black population had been wiped out, though descendants of intermarriage survive today on the islands of Bass Strait, between Tasmania and Australia. When the last surviving man, William Lanney (or Lanné) died in 1869 his body was gruesomely mutilated, apparently to foil would-be body-snatchers. The last woman, Trucanini (there are several other spellings) died seven years later. She was 73, and her life-span exactly covered the years of her people's extermination. Her uncle had been shot by a soldier; her sister, abducted by sealers; her mother, stabbed. Her husband's hands had been chopped off. Her dying words were: 'Don't let them cut me up. Bury me behind the mountains.' But for many years her skeleton was on public display in Hobart Museum. Her remains have now been cremated.[2]

Australia

In Australia, too, the black inhabitants gave valuable help to the earliest white explorers in all parts of the continent. But they soon found to their cost that the subsequent European invasion brought intense and endless suffering. The first destruction was accidental: the introduction of smallpox in 1789. Then the white settlers came:

> It is significant ... that the settlement of Australia occurred ... when the Industrial Revolution was in full swing, with Britain the heart of it. Britishers, from the first discovery that Australian grass could be very profitably turned into fine wool, consistently brushed aside in practice Aboriginal 'rights' when there was money to be made, at the same time condemning the fecklessness of the 'native' who became a poverty-stricken hanger-on on what had been his own land ...
>
> The Australian grasslands were proved a major resource for the industrial technology of England. The sale of the first few bales of fine Merino wool from Sydney made more inevitable a rapid dispossession of the Aboriginal through wide areas of the colony, a brushing aside of the feeble gestures by governors and the British government at traditional colonial administration, and a relegation of Aboriginal resistance from the status of defence of tribal lands to that of wasteful depredation of the wealth of the colony.[3]

White settlers grabbed the good land, driving away indigenous animals, eating or trampling plant life, and pushing black Australians into mountainous, swampy or arid territories. The invaders disrupted ceremonial and religious life, desecrated sacred sites, daubed cave paintings with graffiti, stole sacred stone tablets. They raped and abducted black women, whom they kept chained up like dogs. In direct conflict they killed at least 20,000 black people; between 2,000 and 2,500 Europeans are thought to have died in this fighting. Black Australians were destroyed without mercy, in three main ways: sharp-shooting; poisoning with arsenic or strychnine, usually mixed into flour; and punitive expeditions, the earliest of which was mounted in 1790. Settlers would surround a camp at night, attack at dawn, and slaughter men, women and children indiscriminately. They 'thought no more of shooting a native than shooting a crow'.[4] But many more black Australians died from the invasion's secondary effects: disease, disruption and starvation. Economic dispossession was so complete that in the continent's dry centre more people are thought to have died of starvation, directly and indirectly, than from disease or being shot. Australia's black population fell from about 300,000 in 1788 to 77,501 in 1921, the first year in which a careful census was taken. And those 77,000 were living in conditions of abject pauperism. In 1932 there were 59,719 black Australians. During the next 30 years the decline was halted, but only very gradually: in 1961 the black Australian population numbered 75,309, marginally less than it had been 40 years before.

Even before open conflict ended, the invaders had turned their attention to devising ways of making black Australians work for them. In Perth in the 1840s, the government decreed that black people would be allowed to enter the town only if they were wearing a woollen shirt that had to be earned by labour. Black Australians were placed in reserves managed by white superintendents, and were forbidden to leave. They were liable to forcible removal from one reserve to another. Those who moved to fringe settlements in country towns, and were dependent on the economy of those towns, including persons of mixed parentage, experienced discrimination that kept them miserably poor and prone to disease. Though black people provided an essential supply of labour over much of central and northern Australia they were paid, in 1939, extremely low wages – and often no wages at all, simply hand-outs of poor-quality clothing and food consisting largely of offal. Their housing, when it existed, was often scandalous. In Western Australia, too, many black people endured what has been called 'a mongrel-dog existence in the rubbish heaps of towns'.[5] As late as the 1960s, as the above population figures suggest, black Australians still had one of the highest infant mortality rates in the world.

Not only did the law restrain the movements of black Australians and control their places of residence; in Queensland, for many years, they needed special permission to get married. Children were often permanently taken away from their parents. Elsewhere in northern Australia black men and women arrested as suspects or witnesses were walked to the court-house behind a pack-horse, chained by the neck. Retention of the neckchain was strongly defended by a minister of the interior, H. V. Johnson, as late as 1949.

The Australian system of segregation and repression closely resembled the *apartheid* laws of South Africa, though it received far less publicity. And it was largely supported by the white labour movement. The Australian Workers' Union refused to admit black Australians to membership for many years and in 1924 specifically asked the Arbitration Court to restrict their employment.[6]

New Zealand

British sovereignty over New Zealand was proclaimed in 1840 and systematic European colonization began in the same year. Unlike black Tasmanians and Australians, the Maoris were subsistence gardeners living in settled villages. Their social organization enabled them to mount a formidable resistance to European invasion, and the settlers had to call in British troops to overcome that resistance. Before this military defeat the Maoris had been so powerful that the settlers were forced to negotiate with them to satisfy an 'insatiable appetite' for land.[7] Large promises were made to the Maoris and shamefully broken.

The settlement of New Zealand was organized by the New Zealand Company, which has been described as 'a characteristic product of the City of London'.[8] The company's first chairman was England's biggest individual shipowner; its principal agent described himself as 'half a missionary' but took care to issue his surveyors with swords and pistols rather than Bibles. The 1840 Treaty of Waitangi confirmed the Maori chiefs in the possession of all their lands, and when it was signed the British representative made the fulsome declaration that 'we are now one people'. But it was a gigantic fraud, for the New Zealand Company soon found means to whittle away the treaty's guarantees.

Clever lawyers explained that the treaty didn't really mean what it seemed to mean. It emerged that until a Crown grant had been issued for any piece of land the Maori owner had no standing in a court of law. The only way a chief could acquire enforceable rights over land was by selling it to the Crown and buying it back. If he wasn't satisfied with the price offered by the Crown he couldn't sell it to anybody else. In case of a dispute with the Crown in connection with a sale, no court would listen to a Maori claim. To be sure, the treaty granted the chiefs 'all the rights and privileges of British subjects'; but the lawyers explained that such rights and privileges didn't include any right to their lands. (Nor did they include the right to vote: chiefs' applications to have their names placed on the electoral roll were all rejected on the ground that their dwellings were not built on land bought from the Crown.) In 1844 a House of Commons Select Committee accepted the view that Maori title to land did not extend beyond village sites and cultivations, and that the rest should be declared Crown land and made available for European settlement. And Lord Stanley, after five years of circumlocution by the Colonial Office, ruled that the degree of consideration to be given to Maori 'subjects' was to be modified whenever it clashed with the peace and welfare of European settlers. In short, the Maoris were shamefully cheated.

The New Zealand Company was enabled to buy millions of acres of Maori land for prices ranging from a farthing to three-halfpence an acre. Promises were made involving schooling and medical attention, but in 1868 the clever lawyers again found ways in which the authorities could wriggle out of keeping those promises.

By 1892 the Maoris held less than one-sixth of the country that had once been theirs, and most of the land they did retain was remote, rugged and bush-clad. In the words of *The Oxford History of New Zealand* (1981):

> The main agricultural producers of the 1840s and 1850s, they were now relegated to a precarious subsistence on the fringe of a rapidly expanding European agricultural economy. Maoris ... relied increasingly on seasonal labour on European farms and public works ... Their living conditions were appalling. Most of them lived in makeshift camps, without sanitation.[9]

The Maori population was estimated at between 125,000 and 175,000 before the British invasion; by the turn of the century it had dwindled to an estimated 45,000. Part of the decline was caused by warfare, part by disease. In one year alone (1854) 4,000 Maoris died of measles.

White New Zealanders justified the effects of the European invasion and appropriation of Maori land by telling each other that the Maoris were incorrigibly dirty, lazy savages who could not farm the land profitably and were doomed to extinction. 'Their extermination is to be looked for almost within our own lifetime', wrote a future prime minister of New Zealand in 1851.[10] A compassionate medical man said five years later: 'All we can do is smooth the pillow of the dying Maori race.'[11] Another medical man told the Wellington Philosophical Society in 1882: 'The disappearance of the race is scarcely subject for much regret. They are dying out in a quick, easy way, and are being supplanted by a superior race.'[12] As late as 1907 a New Zealand archdeacon said there could be no doubt that the Maoris were 'rapidly passing away'.[13]

When these prophecies failed to come true, white New Zealanders began to claim that their treatment of the Maoris had been exceptionally satisfactory. This myth accorded with neither the historical facts nor the condition of the Maoris on the eve of the Second World War. In the late 1930s the Maori death rate was 24.31 per 1,000, compared with 9.71 among white New Zealanders. The Maori infant mortality rate was more than 4 times that of whites. There were over 5 times as many Maori deaths from influenza, about 3 times as many from bronchitis, over 4 times as many from pneumonia, and 39 times as many from typhoid. The survival of the Maoris, and of their language and culture, owes nothing to successive New Zealand administrations and everything to their own courage and tenacity.[14]

Southern Africa

South Africa has an exceptionally complex history. It was settled by Dutch as well as British colonists, and there was a complicated and shifting pattern of conflict involving those two groups as well as Bantu-speaking people and the San ('Bushmen') and Khoikhoi ('Hottentots') who were the Cape Province's original inhabitants. A small Dutch colony was established at the Cape of Good Hope in 1652; in the eighteenth century many of the descendants of the Dutch colonists became migrant farmers ('Trek-Boers'), who eventually called themselves Afrikaners. The Cape came under British control during the Anglo-French wars of 1793–1815, but British colonialism did not become the dominant force in southern Africa until the 1870s.

Meanwhile, however, what was later known as *apartheid* originated in the 'Native Reserves' policy of the British administrator Sir Theophilus Shepstone, who served as diplomatic agent in Natal, 1845–53, and Secretary for Native Affairs, 1853–75. During his first four years in Natal, an overwhelmingly British settlement, he 'persuaded' most of the African inhabitants to move into the locations. Thus was born a system whereby Africans performed the manual work for most of the white settlers – on their farms, in their towns and villages, and in their houses – at extremely low wages.[15] Shepstone spent over 30 years shaping Natal's 'racial' policy. He put into operation the first large-scale segregation policy ever attempted, so that by 1860 some 80,000 Africans were settled in 'Native Reserves'.[16] Having toyed at first with the idea of clearing Natal of its 'natives' – a popular concept among the British settlers, provided that enough Africans were left behind to satisfy the need for labour – Shepstone master-minded the establishment of segregated locations for Africans in Natal. A commission appointed in 1846 established eight locations with a total area of 1,168,000 acres.[17] Three years later the British colonial secretary, Earl Grey, laid down a South African policy that stressed the need for drawing labour supplies from the African communities and anticipated that the location system would force Africans to work for the white settlers. In a dispatch to Sir H. G. Smith, governor of the Cape, Earl Grey wrote:

> I regard it ... as desirable that these people should be placed in circumstances in which they should find regular industry necessary for their subsistence ... Every encouragement should ... be afforded to the younger natives to become servants in the families of the European settlers ... Any native who may have quitted his location to reside elsewhere ... would become amenable to the general law of the district; but he should not be allowed to leave the location without a pass, and I concur in [the] suggestion, that each adult male should be distinguished by a plate or medal, with the number of the station to which they may belong.

It was Earl Grey's own suggestion that enough space be left between the 'locations' to permit the spread of white settlements, in order that 'each European emigrant would thus have it in his power to draw supplies of labour from the location in his immediate proximity'.[18] Summing up British policy in Natal, Earl Grey wrote in 1853 that if Africans:

> could be made to exchange their barbarous habits for those of civilized life, the presence of these people would be the greatest possible advantage to the Colonists, by affording them a supply of labour, which is urgently required, and which alone is wanting to render a territory possessing remarkable natural advantages productive ... These people would also ... create a demand for articles of European manufacture which would increase both the trade and revenue of the Colony.[19]

Between the middle and the end of the nineteenth century a series of Bantu kingdoms was subjected to white control. The Xhosa, Griqua, Nguni, Zulu, Sotho, Tswana, Swazi, Mpondo, and Venda were all subjugated, by one means or another. The Xhosa, for instance, were 'driven to desperation' and 'broken' by the drastic land settlement plans of Sir George Grey, governor of the Cape Colony, 1853–59.[20] Some of the conquered communities were divided into small groups and distributed among Afrikaner farmers as 'apprentices'. Often there was fierce resistance, but the colonialists did not always use the method of military confrontation and conquest. Sometimes they contrived to divide and rule. In the case of the Swazi, concessions were used, a kind of economic warfare whereby land and mineral rights were bought, and the king and his council were persuaded to sign away the whole country and all rights over future development, so that, as the Swazi say, it was the 'documents that killed us'.[21] Sometimes, as with the final stage in the subjection of the Mpondo, in the eastern Cape Colony, a mere show of overwhelming military superiority was enough. What happened to the Mpondo in 1894 is described by one of Cecil Rhodes's biographers:

> Rhodes travelled down to Pondoland in a coach and eight cream-coloured horse, some machine-guns and eight policemen, announced that he proposed to annex Pondoland, and sent for Sigcau [the king]. He then offered to show Sigcau what would happen to him and his tribe if there was any further unpleasantness, took him to where the machine-guns were trained on a mealie-field, opened fire on the mealies, and brought down the crop.
>
> Sigcau noted the lesson, and ceded his country.[22]

One historian has written of the Mpondo that 'in the nature of things a petty barbarous government could not be permitted to do what it pleased, even within the limits of its own territory, in opposition to the interests of a powerful civilised neighbour'.[23] On which Leonard Thompson comments, in *The Oxford History of South Africa* (1969–71): 'This is a most revealing statement of the doctrine that might is right – especially when it is white ... The Mpondo ... constituted a potential threat to British supremacy in South Africa. They were therefore subjected.'[24]

But most of the southern African communities were subjected by force: by scorched-earth campaigns meant to deprive the Africans of all means of independent livelihood.[25] For these were not only land wars but also labour wars. Black people lost free access to the land, on which they were permitted to remain only as labourers, herdsmen, tenants or renters.

The discovery of diamonds in 1864 and gold in 1886 dramatically changed the economy of southern Africa. From being almost wholly agricultural, it became predominantly industrial and urban. Black agriculture was undermined, and the black agricultural population was diverted into the service of the European community, now not only in agriculture but also in mining. The officials who administered Britain's share of southern Africa at the turn of the century had no doubt at all about their aims, and they allotted to black people a wholly menial and subordinate role. Black people would do the hard work, primarily in the diamond and gold mines; white people would reap the profits and do the governing. In 1899 Britain's high commissioner in South Africa, Sir Alfred (afterwards Lord) Milner, wrote in a 'very confidential' letter that 'the *ultimate* end is a self-governing white Community, supported by *well-treated* and *justly governed* black labour from Cape Town to Zambesi'. Two years later – in a dispatch to Joseph Chamberlain, the colonial secretary – Milner wrote of Africans: 'Undoubtedly the greatest benefit that could be bestowed on them or South Africa generally would be to teach them habits of regular and skilled labour ... The more natives that are engaged in mining and other industrial pursuits the better for them and for the country.'[26] In a memorandum to General Smuts, entitled 'Notes on a Suggested Policy towards Coloured People and Natives', Lord Selborne, high commissioner for South Africa and governor of the Transvaal and Orange River Colony from 1905 to 1910, discussed the establishment of a hierarchical structure that would ensure a cheap labour supply. Government objectives must include 'the gradual destruction of the tribal system' and 'teaching the Natives to work ... continually and effectively'. Lord Selborne added: 'There can be no surer way of teaching them to work than by increasing their wants, and especially the wants of the women.'[27]

Skill and high wages were seen as privileges of white workers. Heavy labour and menial tasks were left to black workers. The black population was seen as a reservoir of labour for the mines, the towns and the European farms.

The determining factor in early twentieth-century South Africa was not the Anglo–Boer War of 1899–1902, a war fought for possession of some of the world's richest gold mines, but the consolidation of the *apartheid* system. The British had already laid the foundations of this system of racial segregation and oppression. And it was they who now locked the system in place, not the Afrikaners, as is commonly supposed: *apartheid*'s 'ideological and future legislative shape was first modelled by the British rather than the Afrikaners, who were not a significant political force at the time'.[28] The key document in the process was the report of the South African Native Affairs Commission, appointed by Lord Milner, which sat in 1903–5 with Sir Godfrey Lagden in the chair. Lagden, a civil servant and a director of the South African Gold Trust:

saw white supremacy as axiomatic, and race and colour as legitimate differentials in granting political rights; he saw the African as a wage labourer rather than as a peasant farmer. He envisaged an economic colour bar and pass laws to regulate an adequate cheap black labour force. Two features were clearly set forth in the report. First, the principle of territorial segregation, with reserves set apart for Africans, and the racially exclusive and final delimitation of land areas. Secondly, there was to be political separation too ... Not only was the Commission made up entirely of British members, the Report was received with scarcely a murmur of protest either in Britain or South Africa.[29]

The notorious Natives Land Act of 1913, which gave *apartheid* the force of law, was wholly based on Lagden's principles: 'the British government admitted as much in 1913, and no responsible historian will now deny that the guiding principles of the Union's policy specifically and precisely emanated from this Report and this Act.'[30] The Act's primary object was to lay down the principle of territorial segregation. It divided the country into white and 'native' areas. It made it illegal for a black person to buy land outside the reserves, which constituted about 13 per cent of the country's total area, or even to live on a farm except as a servant employed by a white person. This meant that over three-quarters of the population were limited to just over one-eighth of the land. The Act's immediate effect was to uproot masses of black South Africans from white-owned farms and send them wandering round the country looking for somewhere to live. Many were forced to sell off their stock for a song. 'Few laws passed in South Africa can have been felt with such immediate harshness by so large a section of the population.'[31] Black South Africans, whose opposition to the Act was 'vehement and articulate', saw it as a violation of promises made to them by the British government.[32]

For most white people in South Africa, then as now, black Africans were merely units of labour 'whose presence was essential but only tolerable so long as they ministered to the needs of the white man'.[33]

Indentured Labour

Another aspect of the inhuman treatment of black people in the so-called Dominions should not be forgotten: the use of indentured labour from the Indian sub-continent and the Pacific islands. Between 1863 and 1904 Queensland in Australia recruited 62,565 Melanesians from the Loyalty Islands, New Hebrides and Solomon Islands to work on sugar plantations. They were usually housed in large barracks, and 'orders were given and put into effect in a military manner, with parades, drill and vigorous supervision being an essential component of day-to-day life'.[34] In the 1860s Indian indentured labourers began arriving in Natal in South Africa to work on the sugar plantations, and they soon became special objects of white hostility, victims of a succession of restrictive laws, and recipients of numerous illegal floggings. There were in fact so many instances of illegal floggings of Indians in Natal, writes Maureen Tayal, 'that it is reasonable to conclude that the threat of force was ever present, and that the exact nature and extent of that threat was clearly understood by every labourer, and that this understanding was a key element in the maintenance of submissiveness'. By the end of the century there were about 100,000 Indians in Natal.[35]

Indian indentured labour was also used by the British in Malaya,[36] Fiji[37] and Mauritius, where Indian immigration was described as the 'sheet-anchor of colonial prosperity'.[38]

7
Profits of Empire

The British Empire was above all else a mechanism for providing British capitalism with cheap raw materials, land and labour. Given a free hand, wrote Richard Pares, historian of the Caribbean, a 'mother country' will make the kind of empire it needs: 'This is particularly true of the British Empire, because England, more than any other country, has had such a free hand.'[1] So the colonies where black people lived became bases for the production and export of minerals and crops. Each area was made to specialize in the production of one or two commodities. Jamaica produced sugar and bananas; Ceylon, tea and rubber; the Gold Coast, cocoa; the Gambia, groundnuts; Zanzibar, cloves; Tanganyika, sisal and coffee. The minerals were dug by low-paid workers in British-owned mines. The crops were produced either by low-paid workers on British-owned plantations or by peasants whose crops were bought up as cheaply as possible by the monopolies. The latter profited in several distinct ways. They profited from investments in mines and plantations; from buying up cheaply the raw materials produced by the peasants; from selling their manufactured goods in closed colonial markets; from shipping and other services; and from banking and insurance activities in the colonies. So, for British industry and commerce, the colonies were extremely profitable appendages. There is every justification for calling the profits they yielded super-profits.[2]

In short, British capitalists added enormously to their wealth by robbing black people. They robbed them as workers, as peasants, and as consumers. For the great majority of black people who lived in it, the British Empire meant chronic poverty, chronic hunger, disease, atrocious housing, illiteracy and tyranny.

The profitability of the British Empire was frankly admitted by those statesmen who were proud, as many were, to call themselves imperialists. Lord Lugard, one of the Empire's chief architects and theorists, declared in 1893 that the scramble for Africa was due to 'the growing commercial rivalry, which brought home to the civilised nations the vital necessity of securing the only remaining fields for industrial enterprise and expansion'. Britain's imperial responsibilities had been undertaken 'for our ***advantage***' (his emphasis). The object of colonial expansion was 'to foster the growth of the trade of this country and to find an outlet for our manufactures'.[3] The future Liberal prime minister Lord Rosebery put it a little differently in the same year. Britain was engaged in 'pegging out claims for the future', he said, and 'we have to consider, not what we want now, but what we shall want in the future'.[4] Two years later Joseph Chamberlain, the Birmingham screw-manufacturer and ex-radical who served as colonial secretary from 1895 to 1903, declared that Britain's colonies were 'estates' to be developed by 'the judicious investment of British money'.[5]

Of course, as will be seen in Part II, the imperialists also made grandiose claims about the civilizing mission that God had entrusted to them: to rescue black people from backwardness, barbarism, and heathenism. But colonialism's economic advantages were never denied, and were often trumpeted.

8
How Black People were Ruled

How were black people governed in Britain's colonies? The administrative branch of the Colonial Service has been described as 'an elitist corps'.[1] These officials' outstanding attribute was self-assurance: a self-assurance so smug, arrogant and conservative that A. P. Thornton calls it 'a principal foundation of the British Empire'. British colonies, he writes, were 'politically and socially controlled by a handful of highly-trained white men (and their untrained wives) in an atmosphere wherein any advocacy of change was thought equivalent to Bolshevism'. These officials took it for granted that their own 'paternalistic presence' in each particular territory 'would be needed for as long a future as imagination could conjure up'.[2]

For 25 years the person in charge of recruitment to the Colonial Service was Major Sir Ralph Furse, KCMG, DSO, etc. A product of Eton, Balliol and the cavalry, Furse knew that the best sign that an applicant might make a good colonial administrator was the term 'School Prefect' or, better still, 'Head Prefect' in his public school record. After all:

> leading fags at school was like leading natives in Africa or Asia ... One form of paternalism led naturally to another ... Another Public school-imbued characteristic of colonial civil servants was their aloofness from the people they ruled ... To the adolescent English male of the civil service class his Public School was the institutional embodiment of the unspoken class ethic. When he became a colonial official he naturally took his class assumptions and practices with him ... Officials found native aristocrats worthy of one kind of treatment and other natives worthy of another ... The attitude of officials ... was not unlike that which they maintained from childhood towards the lesser orders at home.[3]

But the colonial officials trained for their task in British public schools were not only paternalistic, aloof, and class-biased. They were trained also to be unadaptable, 'unreceptive to criticism and unimaginative in the face of changing circumstances ... It was the native who had to adapt.'[4]

Black people in the British colonies were indeed expected to 'adapt' cheerfully to very unpleasant, and sometimes quite bizarre, behaviour on the part of their white rulers. E. K. Lumley, a British district officer in Tanganyika for many years, relates in his memoirs how he boxed the ears of a black man who wouldn't take his hat off: 'I was only then informed that he was the African priest of the local Lutheran mission.'[5] A district commissioner in the same territory:

> was in the habit of going for a long walk every evening, wearing a hat. When, towards sunset, he came to the point of turning for home we would hang his hat on a convenient tree and proceed on his way back hatless. The first African who passed that way after him and saw the hat was expected to bring it to D.'s house and hand it to his servants, even if he was going in the opposite direction with a long journey ahead of him. If he ignored the hat, he would be haunted by the fear that D.'s intelligence system would catch up with him. I did not believe this story until I myself went for a walk one evening while D. was still in charge, and saw the hat hanging on a tree.[6]

Much the same 'adaptation' was expected of Britain's colonial subjects in India. There was a long tradition of arrogant and brutal behaviour towards the Indians by English officials and other residents. In 1837 the judge Frederick Shore, who had spent 15 years in Bengal, lamented 'the haughty superciliousness, arrogance, and even insolence of behaviour, which the generality of the English think it necessary to adopt towards the natives, by way of keeping up their own dignity'. He went on:

> One would suppose the principle adopted was, to treat the people as a degraded, inferior race. This feeling at least shows itself daily, and pervades, more or less, every thought and action. Few Englishmen return the salute of a native; they can hardly bring themselves to speak to them civilly. The slightest fault of a servant is visited, if not, as is frequently the case, with blows, with the most gross abuse ... Servants are frequently beaten and turned away without paying their wages.[7]

The politician Sir Charles Dilke, visiting India in the 1860s, found this 'significant notice' in all the hotels: 'Gentlemen are earnestly requested not to strike the servants.' He also found that the prospect of enriching themselves through looting was a favourite topic of conversation among 'our men in India'.[8] The journalist James Routledge told in 1878 how he had seen Englishmen elbowing their way through the Indian crowds 'as through a herd of cattle': 'We count men as of an inferior race, deny them careers, and then talk of them as incapable of a higher life.'[9] 'It is painful', wrote H. J. S. Cotton in *New India* (1885) 'to observe the habitual and almost universal exhibition of race insolence displayed by our fellow-countrymen.' English officials had 'assaulted respectable residents of the country because on passing a European in the road they have not dismounted from their horses in token of their inferiority'. British officials referred to Indians as 'niggers', while, among their wives, 'the abuse of "those horrid natives" is almost universal'.[10] Queen Victoria privately condemned the '*snobbish* and vulgar overbearing and offensive behaviour' of many British officials in India, who treated her subjects as 'fit only to be cursed and shot down'.[11]

At public schools the prefects learnt to cane their fags, and some of them learnt to enjoy it; and those who became colonial administrators made much use of flogging to encourage the 'natives' to adapt to their rule. While Joseph Chamberlain was colonial secretary 'malingering' was an offence punishable by flogging in Bechuanaland, as was petty theft among juveniles in Jamaica and 'committing nuisances' in the Gold Coast.[12] Chamberlain did his best to curtail this practice, describing it in 1897 as 'neither more nor less than a gross and discreditable scandal'. He told his officials:

> Flogging is neither more nor less than the application of torture as a punitive proceeding ... All experience shows that the European authority is only too ready to inflict a punishment of this kind, which costs nothing, causes him no trouble or compunction, and gratifies his sense of personal power and superiority. The liability to abuse in these cases, therefore, is very great.[13]

Little seems to have been done, however. In 1907 the president of the Kenya Colonists' Association, Ewart Grogan, took the leading role in the 'most brutal' public flogging of three Kikuyus in front of the Nairobi court-house, to assert his right to do as he pleased with 'his' Africans.[14] And in 1912 the Zaria scandal in northern Nigeria, when two black railway clerks were publicly flogged for failing to prostrate themselves before a petty British official, was also publicized in Britain. But as Ian Duffield has pointed out, the public flogging of Africans in the nude, women as well as men, on the orders of British officials, was so common in that period that only the most flagrant examples attracted attention.[15] Some of the worst cases of brutality and flagrant abuse of power took place on mission stations, where missionaries were at times given to inflicting 'remarkably severe floggings'.[16]

9
The Empire and the British Working Class

Economic advantage through the exploitation of black people was not the only way in which the British Empire was of value to the British ruling class. It was of value to them in three other ways, too.

In the first place, the imperialists were deeply anxious about social unrest and possible revolution in Britain, and they saw in the expansion of Empire and the exploitation of the colonies a way of ensuring prosperity and damping down unrest, so preserving their rule. If the British working class could be convinced that it was sharing in the benefits of colonialism, its discontent would be lessened. Moreover the Empire would directly reduce unemployment by furnishing both an outlet for Britain's allegedly surplus population and a series of new markets. The journalist W. T. Stead, in a work of fiction called *The History of the Mystery* (1896), attributed this view to 'the Right Hon. R. T. Cecil', a transparent disguise for Stead's friend Cecil Rhodes, the unscrupulous adventurer who gave his name to part of conquered Africa. The unemployed, said 'Cecil', were crying out for bread; the British people's very existence depended on the Empire; the 'Imperial question' was a bread-and-butter question.[1] Rhodes's fellow-imperialist Joseph Chamberlain held similar views:

> Like many other European leaders of his day, Chamberlain had a profound fear of social revolution. If the fluctuations in the economy were not modified by conscious government policies to combat economic recession, Chamberlain feared a possible breakdown in the economic system, bringing in its train class warfare and social chaos. The way to avoid these dangers, he believed, was to make the country prosperous by a far-seeing policy of colonial expansion and development.[2]

In the second place, the super-profits derived from exploitation of black people in the colonies enabled the British capitalist class, not merely to give certain benefits to the 'aristocracy of labour' (the better-paid 15 per cent of the working class) from about the middle of the nineteenth century, but also, in time, to give sectional benefits to some of the lower-paid workers too. However badly Scottish miners were paid in the 1930s, they could earn in an hour or two the shilling that it took a Nigerian miner a whole six days to earn.

The third social consequence of colonialism in Britain was the emergence of a large stratum of white-collar workers, both male and female. This new 'aristocracy of labour', socially and politically hardly less conservative than the old, staffed the vastly expanded offices needed for running a capitalist empire. What the Maxim gun was to the imperial army, the typewriter (first marketed in 1876) was to this army of clerks on whom the system depended for its communications and records.

Inevitably, therefore, colonialism helped to create social circumstances highly favourable to its wide acceptance in Britain. Public enthusiasm for the British Empire was whipped up by the churches; by the schools (free compulsory education was introduced in 1870); by the comics and adventure stories produced for children and young people ('a tremendous expansion in the publication of juvenile literature occurred in the 1870s and 1880s');[3] by the new cheap and sensationalist press (the first halfpenny London daily was launched in 1896); and by music halls, popular plays, musical comedies and popular songs. These were the main transmission belts for the mythology of imperial glory and heroism and of racial superiority.

Within the working-class movement the leaders of the Labour Party and trade unions were not so much a transmission belt for such ideas (though this was one of their functions) as an obstacle to the emergence of any real challenge to them or questioning of them. Most of the Labour leaders were not merely totally uninformed about the Empire but totally devoid of interest in it. They shared in the fruits of colonialism and had little desire or incentive to find out how those fruits were grown and gathered. They shared the profound ignorance of almost all MPs – indeed, of almost all inhabitants of metropolitan Britain – concerning every aspect of the Empire. This was not merely the case in the nineteenth century, when at least one MP thought British Guiana was an island.[4] It has equally been the case in the twentieth century, at every social level. A public opinion survey by the Colonial Office in 1949 found that over half of a representative sample of the population was unable to name a single British colony.[5] And when colonial estimates were discussed the House of Commons was invariably deserted.[6] Labour MPs' 'negligence and lack of initiative', fully shared by the trade union leaders, led them – with very few exceptions – to ignore the Empire and the condition of its subject peoples.[7] The general socialist attitude was 'an abhorrence of colonial wars, a condescending attitude to non-European civilisations and an implicit assumption of leadership'.[8] Even the revolutionary socialist H. M. Hyndman called himself 'an Imperialist' who 'believed in the beneficent influence of the British flag and the glories of British rule all over the world, considering, indeed, that our expansion was good alike for governors and governed'.[9]

Since Labour leaders were both ignorant and primarily concerned with amassing votes, some of them:

> accepted the idea that the possession of empire was important to the interests of the working classes, or that it was an inevitable obligation which had to be fulfilled in as ethical a manner as possible. To attack the possession of colonies seemed to be unpatriotic, and therefore electorally dangerous.[10]

It is said that when Labour first took office in 1924 J. H. Thomas, the former railway worker who was appointed colonial secretary, introduced himself to his heads of departments with the statement: 'I'm here to see that there is no mucking about with the British Empire.'[11] Any sort of colonial policy, let alone an anti-colonialist one, was very slow to develop within the Labour Party. Moreover, even 'those who spelt out the case for a positive colonial policy for socialists could not avoid a sense of racial superiority'.[12] *Fabianism and the Empire* (1900), a pamphlet drafted and edited by Bernard Shaw, justified Britain's conquest of the Transvaal and declared that 'the British Empire, wisely governed, is invincible'.[13] Lord Rosebery, praised by Sidney Webb, a leading Fabian, for having an imperial outlook, admired this pamphlet and 'sent various gracious messages to the Shaws'.[14] The Fabians, who 'apparently regarded it as justifiable for a country of "higher civilization" to take over "backward" countries', took no further interest in the Empire for many years;[15] the Fabian Colonial Bureau was not founded until 1940. A policy of 'Empire Socialism', first advocated by Thomas Johnston, editor of *Forward*, was adopted by George Lansbury's *Labour Weekly* group in 1925, and that year's Labour Party conference passed a resolution in favour of it. Some Labour MPs formed a Labour Commonwealth Group in the 1920s; its aim was merely to change the Empire from a 'boss-controlled Empire', making use of cheap labour, to 'a Labour-controlled commonwealth, in which we are the directors of policy'.[16]

Historians disagree about how far the British working class gave enthusiastic support to colonialism, and the evidence is certainly hard to assess. As Robert Gray has pointed out, 'indifferent or even critical attitudes to empire and opposition to particular imperial adventures could be quite compatible with a deeper sense of national superiority and complicity in the maintenance of British imperial supremacy'.[17] And without doubt many workers, when they thought about the matter at all, did regard the British Empire as somehow their own. They believed what they were told: that British rule was bringing peace, fairness, justice and civilization to peoples who would otherwise know only strife, tyranny, injustice and barbarism; and that if Britain's Empire were not strengthened and expanded, those of other European powers would be. They accepted Rosebery's view that the Empire was God's will and that in British success in expanding it everyone 'must see the finger of the Divine'.[18] They accepted Curzon's view that the British Empire was 'the greatest instrument for good that the world has seen'.[19] They accepted without question the assurance that black people 'nearly always welcome British rule, and cheerfully submit to it'.[20] They accepted, in short, the 'scientific' racism which evolved as a justification of colonialism and whose essential message was that black people were, for one reason or another, unfit to rule themselves.

Among a minority in the British working-class movement, however, there was a tradition of opposition to colonialism and of solidarity with the oppressed peoples within the British Empire. Associated with this tradition were the Independent Labour Party, Communist Party (in its earlier years), League against Imperialism, and Movement for Colonial Freedom.

Part II
Racism

10

The Concept of 'Race'

The concept of 'race' is pre-scientific and pseudo-scientific. It belongs to the prehistory of the biological sciences. For the past 30 or 40 years geneticists and anthropologists, when discussing the variations in human physical characteristics, have tended to avoid this concept. They have discarded it as 'artificial' and 'meaningless',[1] 'obsolete' and 'almost mystical',[2] 'out-of-date, if not irrational',[3] 'a particularly virulent term',[4] 'a facet of the folklore of Western civilization that is inadequate to account for the facts of human biological variation'.[5] The American anthropologist Ashley Montagu, who sees the concept of 'race' as one of the greatest and most tragic errors of our time, has suggested that a word which has exercised such an evil tyranny over human minds should be 'permanently dethroned from the vocabulary'.[6] And Frank B. Livingstone, in his 1962 paper 'On the Non-Existence of Human Races', wrote: 'There are no races, there are only clines.'[7]

What is a cline? This term, introduced by Julian Huxley in 1938,[8] denotes a gradation in measurable distinguishing features ('characters') within a species. In human beings one such cline, or 'character gradient', refers to the activities of those cells, known as melanocytes, that produce 'black' pigment (melanin) in skin and hair. Melanin is not itself black; viewed in isolation each single granule of it, measuring anything from one-tenth to two-fifths of a thousandth of a millimetre, is deep golden. It is the piling up of these granules of golden pigment that leads to the absorption of most of the light of all colours that falls on the skin, and so makes the skin of some people appear black.

Now, the cline which measures the activity of pigment-producing cells in human populations, and the consequent wide range of apparent skin and hair colour in human beings, can be correlated with no other human attribute. Skin pigmentation has nothing at all to do with 'civilization', or intelligence, or energy, or creativity, or any kind of skill. And to divide human beings into arbitrary groups called 'races' on the trivial basis of skin pigmentation or some other morphological distinction – i.e. distinction of form – has no scientific validity. All human beings have the same number of chromosomes. All are interfertile. All have blood made up of the same constituents. The so-called 'races' merely represent 'different kinds of temporary mixtures of genetic materials common to all mankind'.[9]

So it impossible to define human 'races' by absolute characteristics. While there are obviously phenotypical variations between human beings (phenotype means the total of the detectable characteristics of an individual or group, as determined by genetic make-up and environmental factors) there is no scientific basis for dividing people into biological groups according to phenotypical factors and attributing fixed cultural attributes to these groups. There is no inherent and immutable association between physical and mental traits, and it is a delusion to suppose that there is. Physical differences do not reflect underlying and significant mental differences, and it is a delusion to suppose that they do. Cultural differences are not biologically determined, and it is a delusion to suppose that they are.

But these delusions, of the kind which have come to be known as racism, are not merely scientific errors, hangovers from the infancy of the biological sciences. For about 300 years racism has had a precise social function. It has functioned as an *ideology*: a system of false ideas justifying the exploitation and domination of people with a visible degree of melanin in their skin by people whose melanocytes are not so active. 'Race', expunged from the vocabulary of scientists, persists in everyday speech as a political category – a category that helps to determine who has power over whom. The ascription of individuals to racial groups is a political act. Racial labels are in fact political weapons by means of which 'a dominant group can retain a subject group in subjection'.[10]

11
Racism and Slavery

Racist ideology sprang from slavery. It arose as a justification of the enslavement of black people in the New World. At the very heart of the new capitalist system that was clawing its way to world supremacy there was a tragic anomaly. This anomaly had three aspects. The rising capitalist class depended for its very existence on free labour; yet it made extensive use of slave labour as its springboard. It harnessed to production a whole series of technological advances; yet it depended extensively on the most backward and inefficient method of production. It proudly inscribed freedom of the individual on its banner; yet it not only 'conquered, absorbed, and reinforced servile labor systems throughout the world' but also 'created new ones, including systems of chattel slavery, on an unprecedented social scale and at an unprecedented level of violence'. This class therefore '*required* a violent racism not merely as an ideological rationale but as a psychological imperative'.[1]

This anomaly found dramatic expression in a famous courtroom scene at the London Mansion House in the year 1767. A young black man called Jonathan Strong had been kidnapped and thrown in jail on behalf of a Jamaica planter. He appealed for help to the anti-slavery campaigner Granville Sharp and was brought before the lord mayor, who ruled that Strong was not guilty of any offence and was therefore free to go. Whereupon the captain of the ship which was to have transported Strong to Jamaica grasped his arm, in open court, and declared that he would secure him as the planter's property. Sharp warned the captain that, if he presumed to take Strong, he would find himself charged with assault. The captain, in Sharp's words, 'withdrew his hand, and all parties retired from the presence of the Lord Mayor, and Jonathan Strong departed also, in the sight of all, in full liberty, nobody daring afterwards to touch him'.[2]

Here, in dramatic collision, are the two basic principles of the new, rising, capitalist world order: property rights; and individual freedom. Five years later, Lord Chief Justice Mansfield would partially restrict the former and partially uphold the latter – not, as the official myth has always claimed, by setting black slaves in Britain free but by ruling that a slave called James Somerset might not lawfully be taken out of England against his will.[3] This was a limited resolution, at the legal level, of that clash between two cardinal principles of the capitalist world outlook which was acted out at the Mansion House in 1767.

But British sugar planters in the Caribbean, and their mouthpieces in Britain, were resolving the contradiction at the ideological level in a very different way. At the Mansion House, the captain referred to Strong as a piece of property. No, retorted Sharp, Strong was a human being and therefore free. If the planter had been there and had spoken his mind he would have said something to this effect: 'This is no human being but a kind of ape or sub-man for which I have undertaken to pay £30 as soon as it is securely on board ship.' That this is no exaggeration is shown by the words of another Jamaica planter, John Gardner Kemeys, who wrote in a pro-slavery pamphlet published in 1783:

> Many of the negroes imported from Africa partake of the brute creation; not long since a cargo of them arrived in Jamaica, whose hands had little or no ball to the thumbs, whose nails were more of the claw kind than otherwise, and their want of intellectual faculties was very apparent. Every planter knows that there are negroes, who ... cannot be humanized as others are, that they will remain, with respect to their understanding, but a few degrees removed from the ouran-outang [i.e. the chimpanzee and gorilla]; and from which many negroes may be supposed, without any very improbable conjecture to be the offspring ... The Colonists of the West-Indies are instrumental in humanizing the descendants of the offspring of even brutes ... to the honour of the human species, and to the glory of the divine being ...
>
> If the controul we maintain over them is proved to be for their good, and to the welfare of society; that it is, probably, taming of brutes ... theirs [*sic*] and our rights will appear in very different points of view.[4]

Just as it was a benefit to the children of the poor to take them away from their miserable and depraved parents, so it was a benefit to Africans to make plantation slaves of them, for they were thereby tamed and humanized. Here is something more than mere cant; here is an ideology, a system of false ideas serving class interests. Here in fact is the earliest stage of racism: plantocracy racism. This ideology can be traced in the planters' oral tradition by the middle of the seventeenth century. It is reported, and convincingly analysed as a class ideology, in *The Negro's & Indians Advocate* (1680) by the Anglican minister Morgan Godwyn.

There was a widespread but false belief that a slave who was baptized was thereby set free. This belief had no doubt been strengthened by court judgments of 1677 and 1694 which suggested that since black people were 'infidels' or 'heathens' they might be treated as property.[5] Ministers of religion who, like Godwyn, visited the Caribbean and told the planters they ought to have their slaves baptized were seen as threatening the planters' property rights. They were told that baptism would be pointless, since slaves were not human beings but animals without souls to save.[6]

Racism first emerged in Britain itself in the eighteenth century. The pivotal figure in its development was the philosopher John Locke, who played a large part in the creation of the Board of Trade, the architect of the old colonial system. As a senior administrator of slave-owning colonies in the New World, Locke helped to draft instructions to the governor of Virginia in which black slavery was regarded as justifiable.[7] Locke's contribution to emerging racism was his provision of a model which allows skin colour to be counted as an essential property of human beings.[8] Racism was openly expressed in the writings of the philosopher David Hume, who also served for a time as a senior administrator of colonial affairs. Black people were, in Hume's opinion, 'naturally inferior' to whites, who held a monopoly of civilization, art, science, and talent.[9] Thus 'the conceptual building blocks which were initially used in the construction of racism ... were largely provided ... by *racist* empiricists.'[10]

The classic expression of plantocracy racism was the *History of Jamaica* (1774) by Edward Long, a former judge and planter on that island. Long adduced 'scientific' evidence for black inferiority, and his *History* was in fact the key text in the turn to the pseudo-scientific racism that served, in the nineteenth and twentieth centuries, as a justification of colonialism.[11]

12
Racism and Empire

By 1914 the British Empire covered 12,700,000 square miles, of which the United Kingdom accounted for less than one-hundredth. It had a population of 431 million, of which the white self-governing population of the UK and the 'Dominions' totalled 60 million, or less than one-seventh. To establish, maintain and justify their rule over, and exploitation of, 370 million black people, Britain's rulers needed a racism more subtle and diversified – but no less aggressive – than the plantocratic variety.

As *phrenology*, racism told the British that they were ruling over peoples who, unlike themselves, lacked force of character. This pseudo-science deduced people's characters from the shape of their skulls. Its practitioners held that the skulls of Africans clearly demonstrated their inferiority to Europeans, and that the inferior races would in time become extinct.

As *teleology*, racism told the British that black people had been put on earth expressly to work for white people, especially in the tropics. This view, held by Thomas Carlyle and Anthony Trollope, was summed up thus in 1865, in the *Spectator*: 'The negroes are made on purpose to serve the whites, just as the black ants are made on purpose to serve the red.'[1]

As *evolutionism*, racism told the British that black people were to be hated, feared, fought and, ultimately, exterminated. This was the view of the Scottish anatomist Dr Robert Knox, as expressed in *The Races of Men* (1850); and of the traveller William Hepworth Dixon, as expressed in *White Conquest* (1876).

As *anthropology*, racism told the British that black people were closer to apes than to Europeans; that they were intellectually inferior to Europeans; that they needed to be humanized, civilized and controlled; and that these tasks could be performed only by white people. The chief nineteenth-century exponent of this variety of racism was James Hunt, founder of the Anthropological Society of London and staunch defender of Governor Eyre of Jamaica in his ferocious suppression of the Jamaican rebellion of 1865 (see pp. 98–100 below).

As *social darwinism*, racism told the British that black people were intellectually inferior to white people and doomed to extinction. This view was propagated by Benjamin Kidd in *Social Evolution* (1894); by Sir Francis Galton, founder of the 'science' of eugenics; and by Galton's pupil Karl Pearson, for whom exterminated inferior races were stepping-stones for the physically and mentally fitter race.[2]

As *Anglo-Saxonism*, racism told the British that God had fitted precisely them to rule over others; that the British constitutional and legal systems were the freest, fairest and most efficient in the world; and that lesser, 'degenerate' races were better dead. This brand of racism, which formed part of the ideological baggage of Carlyle, Arnold, Sir Edward Bulwer-Lytton, Charles Dilke, author of *Greater Britain* (1868), Charles Kingsley and Cecil Rhodes, served in large measure to justify British rule over the Irish. Anglo-Saxonism saw the Irish as 'unstable, childish, violent, lazy, feckless, feminine, and primitive', a view that had first taken definite form in the twelfth century.[3]

In its cosmetic version, as *trusteeship*, racism told the British that they had a duty to promote the moral and educational progress of the child-like 'natives' they ruled over. Since black people were inferior, the British who ruled them owed them a special obligation, not unlike the obligation that decent Englishmen owed to women, children and animals. This was the view of Sir Charles Eliot in *The East Africa Protectorate* (1905) and of Sir F. D. (afterwards Lord) Lugard in *The Dual Mandate in British Tropical Africa* (1922).

In its popular version, transmitted through schools, cheap newspapers, juvenile literature and the music-hall, racism told the British working class that black people were savages whom British rule was rescuing from heathenism and internecine strife.

Of course some of these varieties of racism were more 'scientific' than others. What they all had in common was a political function. All of them, in one way or another, justified British rule over black people. And they were usually jumbled together in the thinking and writing of British politicians, administrators and propagandists of empire, who found endless ways of demonstrating and asserting that black people were unfit to govern themselves. It is fair to say that all these thinkers and writers, with scarcely an exception, were racists. From the 1870s onwards, in Philip D. Curtin's words, 'virtually every European concerned with imperial theory or imperial administration believed that physical racial appearance was an outward sign of inborn propensities, inclinations, and abilities'.[4] From time to time, says Bernard Porter, some of the leading British imperialists 'condemned certain manifestations of racial insolence and intolerance amongst white men in the colonies'. But it does not follow from this that they were not themselves racists. 'They were impressed by "racial" ... differences, and they believed ... that colonial policies should take account of these differences. This was one reason why self-government was supposed to be unsuitable for non-Europeans.'[5]

And not only self-government, but any share, however tiny, in the administration of the British Empire. Until as late as 1942 candidates for the British Colonial Service were required to be of 'pure European descent'.[6] To Cecil Rhodes, as to many others, empire meant the established authority of 'the English-speaking race' over 'the dark-skinned myriads of Africa and Asia'.[7] Comparing the British colonial system with the French, the politician Walter Elliot said in 1922 that the British people would rather lose the whole of their empire than 'submit to a full-blooded ... negro sitting in the House of Lords'.[8] White superiority was something that British colonial administrators took absolutely for granted. One of the ablest of them, Sir Harry Johnston, wrote in a book significantly titled *The Backward Peoples* (1920), that whites were not only the handsomest of the human 'races': they were also the most intelligent and most truthful.[9] In Lord Milner's opinion, black people simply did not possess 'the gift of maintaining peace and order for themselves'; so the idea of extending self-government to India was 'a hopeless absurdity'.[10]

Sir Norman Angell claimed in 1932 that 'British superiority' was deliberately cultivated in India as a theory of government,[11] and there is much evidence to support this claim. Indians were seen as tricky, devious, untruthful, sensuous and easily corrupted. The virtues an Englishman looked for in an Indian friend, if he had one, were loyalty, fidelity and 'spirit' – in short, 'the qualities of a good hound'.[12] Curzon, viceroy of India from 1898 to 1905, spoke of his subjects in terms usually reserved for pet animals; at best they were 'less than schoolchildren'.[13] Balfour, prime minister from 1902 to 1905, was 'an unquestioning believer in white supremacy', and his 'racism ... led him to adopt a negative attitude towards Liberal political reform in India'.[14] One British official in India held in the 1880s that it was 'suicidal' for the British to admit that Indians could do anything better than themselves: 'They should claim to be superior *in everything*, and only allow Natives to take a secondary or subordinate part.'[15] Explaining why Indians must be excluded from the highest ranks of the Indian Civil Service, a 1904 resolution of the Governor General in Council made it clear that only Englishmen possessed:

> partly by heredity, partly by up-bringing, and partly by education, the knowledge of the principles of Government, the habits of mind, and the vigour of character, which are essential for the task ... The rule of India being a British rule, and any other rule being in the circumstances of the case impossible, the tone and standard should be set by those who have created and are responsible for it.[16]

And that was in fact how India was administered. From the central secretariat right down to the district officers, the administration was in the hands of 900 British civil servants.[17]

Such views, as Frances M. Mannsaker has shown, fairly saturated the popular fiction written by 'Anglo-Indians' (English people long resident in India) for consumption by 'Anglo-Indians'. These novels, of which there were not a few, insisted that Indians were incapable of upholding Western principles of integrity, honour and duty. They assumed a belief in British racial supremacy and portrayed Indians as barbarous and savage.[18]

Africans too were seen as racially unfit to govern themselves. The British regarded Africans as dirty, immoral, untruthful, devious, idle, imprudent, impulsive and excitable – an image which 'corresponded almost exactly to the English stereotype of the Irish in the sixteenth century'.[19] The British picture of Africa at the beginning of the twentieth century is summed up by Porter:

> African society was non-society because it was not *their* society; Africans had no artistic culture because there were no cathedral spires in the Kalahari; they were primitive because they were naked and Britons had been naked when *they* were primitive; they had always been 'backward' because they were 'backward' now; if they advanced it would take them centuries because it had taken Europe centuries ... The missionaries in their search for funds played up the 'degradation'; so did administrators and capitalists if it justified their designs ... Africans were not fit to rule themselves.[20]

The 'scientific' view of Africans, as expressed in 1865 by T. H. Huxley, one of the nineteenth century's most respected scientists, was to hold sway for almost 100 years. According to Huxley, no rational man believed that 'the average negro' was the equal of the average white man. It was 'simply incredible' that the black man could 'compete successfully with his bigger-brained and smaller-jawed rival, in a contest which is to be carried on by thoughts and not by bites'. And so 'the highest places in the hierarchy of civilization will assuredly not be within the reach of our dusky cousins'.[21] To Lord Lugard, one of Britain's foremost authorities on colonial administration, the essential point in dealing with Africans was 'to establish a respect for the European', who must assert 'a superiority which commands the respect and excites the emulation of the savage'. The European 'must at all times assert himself, and repel an insolent familiarity ... His dwelling-house should be as superior to those of the native as he is himself superior to them.'[22] A British assistant resident in Nyasaland gave the same advice: 'A wholesome respect for us as beings mysteriously apart from them, infinitely wiser, and above all, infinitely more powerful than they are, is the only key to entire dominion over such people as the aborigines of Central Africa.'[23]

Racism also served as an instrument of white domination in the territories of white settlement. In Australia, racism 'enjoyed many of the trappings of a state religion'. Australia and New Zealand 'had to be kept pure and white'. The discriminatory legislation of Australia, New Zealand, South Africa and Canada assumed that black people were of less value than white; and 'most of the officials in the corridor of power agreed with the racial attitude of the colonists'.[24] And when Balfour, for instance, spoke of racial equality in South Africa it was not black people he had in mind. Indeed, he wrote of the 'inferior black race with whom white men cannot live and work on equal terms', and told the Commons in 1909 that 'to suppose that the races of Africa are in any sense the equals of men of European descent, so far as government, as society, as the higher interests of civilisation are concerned, is really, I think, an absurdity'.[25]

The view that black people were like animals or children – or were indeed 'half animal half children', as the theologian Henry Drummond put it in his book *Tropical Africa* (1888)[26] – and that they therefore needed wise control by white men, was not incompatible with an affectionate though patronizing regard for them. The British assistant resident who fancied himself to be infinitely wiser than the Africans he lorded it over professed also his 'sincere regard' for 'the native': 'I love him somewhat as I love my dog, because he is simple, docile and cheerful.'[27] A *Daily Mail* correspondent in Africa found that 'nigger children, like baby camels, baby wild boars, and baby giraffes, are among the prettiest creatures in the world'.[28]

Other racists were less affectionate. The anthropologist Edward B. Tylor, in his much reprinted classic *Primitive Culture* (1871), held that 'savage moral standards' were 'far looser and weaker than ours', adding: 'We may, I think, apply the often-repeated comparison of savages to children as fairly to their moral as to their intellectual condition.'[29]

The traveller Sir Samuel White Baker, whose family had made its fortune from sugar plantations in Jamaica and Mauritius, went into more detail about black people's moral inferiority. Africans were 'mere apes', 'far below the brutes', and 'disgusting'. Monkeys, indeed, were 'far more civilized than these naked savages'. He 'never saw such scoundrels as Africa produces'. Human nature as viewed among the Africans was 'quite on a level with that of the brute, and not to be compared with the noble character of the dog. There is neither gratitude, pity, love, nor self-denial; no idea of duty; no religion; but covetousness, ingratitude, selfishness and cruelty. All are thieves.' Black people had therefore to be 'specially governed and forced to industry'. The black man was in fact rather like a horse: 'Like a horse without harness, he runs wild, but, if harnessed, no animal is more useful.'[30] The journalist G. W. Steevens, another *Daily Mail* special correspondent, made a different comparison in 1897:

> Niggers are like monkeys ... It is not only their backward sloping foreheads, and huge projecting lips. They squat about the street and jabber like monkeys; they are always pinching each other or trying little tricks, such as throwing up a nut and catching it in the mouth. A black cannot even walk down the street without touching everything laid out before every shop as he passes. I must own that it seems to me awful that such people should have votes.

Steevens was certain however that black people, being so 'happy and lazy, jolly and improvident', were satisfied with their 'proper position of inferiority'.[31] The political essence of his racism was made quite clear when he wrote in the following year about Indian seafarers. After a colourful passage in which he described their teeth 'gleaming devilishly out of demon faces', he came to the heart of the matter: 'It is because there are people like this in the world that there is an Imperial Britain. This sort of creature has to be ruled, so we rule him, for his good and our own.'[32]

The political function of racism is indeed so transparent that it is puzzling, to say the least, to find learned professors of sociology and experts on 'race relations' denying that racism was ever a handmaiden of empire. When Milner, for instance, wrote that Africans 'at best are children, needing and appreciating a just paternal government',[33] this was both 'a sanction and preparation for white control', since its chief implication was to deny Africans the right to govern themselves. When British missionaries, adventurers, politicians and colonial administrators said black people were inferior, 'all such statements helped to justify the undertaking of any European enterprise, religious, economic, or imperial, in which the African was an object ... The imperialist, like the missionary, justified his intervention by placing strong emphasis ... on the backwardness of the African.'[34] Racism served primarily as a device to legitimate British expansion and British rule. 'What is Empire', asked Lord Rosebery in 1900, 'but the predominance of race?'[35]

13
The Reproduction of Racism

Historiography

During the period of empire, racism permeated every field of intellectual life in Britain. In no field was its influence more pervasive, or more pernicious, than historiography. Children and young people were taught a version of history which idealized and glamorized Britain, and portrayed black people as inferior. Most of the respected names in British nineteenth-century historiography were racists, and most of them reflected in their writings one or other of the central tenets of racist ideology. On the work of these giants towering over the subject there were trained several generations of history students, many of whom went on to teach in schools where the history primers reproduced the same racist mythology.

British historical writing in the nineteenth century was 'not only tinged but ... strongly united' with a racism directed against other European peoples as well as against black people.[1] British historians in the nineteenth century were the 'most vigorous proponents' of racism. The dominant note in British historiography before 1914 was 'justification, encouragement, defence and apology for colonies'. And this justification and defence of colonialism were 'profoundly tainted' with racism.[2] These historians glorified the Teutonic 'race'; they expressed downright British chauvinism; and they displayed contempt for 'inferior races'.[3] In a recent survey of these historians' work, J. W. Burrow sums up their major writings as 'like the triumphal arches of a past empire, their vaunting inscriptions increasingly unintelligible to the modern inhabitants: visited occasionally, it may be, as a *pissoir*, a species of visit naturally brief'.[4] And it may well be true that few people nowadays do more than dip into any of these works, many of which are by modern standards formidably long-winded, or formidably pompous, or both. But this should not blind us to the enormous and sustained influence they, and their racism, have had on their successors.

In his famous minute on education for India, Lord Macaulay – whose father Zachary had been British governor of Sierra Leone from 1793 to

1799 – dismissed out of hand India's past achievements, potentialities and languages. Europeans were not merely intellectually superior to Indians; their intellectual superiority was 'absolutely immeasureable'.[5]

James Anthony Froude, who became Regius Professor of Modern History at Oxford, has been described as 'creator of that cult of Elizabethan naval heroism which is with us yet in an attenuated form',[6] as an avowed imperialist, and as 'a leading promoter of the imperialist excitement of the closing years of the nineteenth century'.[7] Froude's *Oceana, or England and her Colonies* (1886) saw England as 'Queen among the nations', pouring into her colonies 'those poor children of hers now choking in fetid alleys'.[8] Following a visit to the Caribbean, Froude wrote *The English in the West Indies* (1888), in which he called black people 'children' and 'mere good-natured animals':

> The poor black was a faithful servant as long as he was a slave. As a freeman he is conscious of his inferiority at the bottom of his heart, and would attach himself to a rational white employer with at least as much fidelity as a spaniel. Like the spaniel, too, if he is denied the chance of developing under guidance the better qualities which are in him, he will drift back into a mangy cur ...
>
> We have a population to deal with, the enormous majority of whom are of an inferior race ... Give them independence, and in a few generations they will peel off such civilisation as they have learnt as easily and as willingly as their coats and trousers.[9]

The great constitutional historian Edward Augustus Freeman, who also became Regius Professor of Modern History at Oxford, subscribed to equally 'violent and unattractive prejudices'.[10] A 'cantankerous and unrepentant Teutonic racialist', Freeman was captivated by the concept of an 'Aryan' race and stock of institutions. 'Near-homogeneity of race' was for him the vital basis of political life.[11] Visiting the United States in 1881, he wrote to a friend: 'This would be a grand land if only every Irishman would kill a negro, and be hanged for it. I find this sentiment generally approved – sometimes with the qualification that they want Irish and negroes for servants, not being able to get any other.' Freeman's 'Aryan prejudices' (his own expression) against 'the niggers who swarm here' made it hard for him to believe that black people were human beings. He saw them as 'big monkeys dressed up for a game' and was sure it had been a mistake to make them citizens. He shivered at the thought 'that one of these great black apes may (in theory) be President. Surely treat your horse kindly; but don't make him consul.'[12]

Another great constitutional historian was William Stubbs. It was he who started the serious study of history in English universities, and he became successively bishop of Chester and of Oxford. John Kenyon writes that 'his shadow still lies across the Oxford School of Modern History in 1980' and that 'some of his most dubious assumptions are still at the roots of our historical thinking'.[13] Eric Williams points out that:

> Stubbs said never a word at any time about slavery, whether medieval or modern ... Certain it is that for a Professor of Modern History at Oxford delivering seventeen annual lectures on the study of medieval and modern history and kindred subjects, under statutory obligation, between the years 1867 and 1884, to make no mention at all of the West Indies, Negro slavery, the abolition movement ... is an achievement of which few men must be capable.[14]

What did interest Bishop Stubbs was the Teutonic origin of English institutions, and the abstract ideas that, as he saw it, various nations represented. Russia represented force; France, 'to some extent', democracy; Turkey, butchery and barbarism. England however represented 'clear-sighted justice and living sympathy with what is good and sound in the progress of the world'.[15]

Lord Acton, who helped to found the *English Historical Review*, planned the *Cambridge Modern History*, and is regarded as 'one of the last of the great Victorian seers',[16] extolled 'the missionary vocation of the English race ... among the nations it has conquered'.[17] According to Acton, the Persians, Greeks, Romans and Teutons were 'the only makers of history, the only authors of advancement'. Other races were 'a negative element in the world; sometimes the barrier, sometimes the instrument, sometimes the material, of those races to whom it is given to originate and to advance'.[18] Following James Mill (who had written of the Indians: 'This people ... are perfectly destitute of historical records'[19]), Acton declared that 'the Hindoos ... have no history of their own, but supply objects for commerce and for conquest'.[20] Referring specifically to the British Empire, Acton held that 'inferior races are raised by living in political union with races intellectually superior'.[21] Slavery was to Acton 'a mighty instrument not for evil only, but for good in the providential order of the world'.[22]

Sir John Robert Seeley, whom Gladstone appointed Regius Professor of Modern History at Cambridge, wrote *The Expansion of England* (1883). This book made such an appeal 'to the pride and patriotism of most English-speaking persons'[23] that it sold over 80,000 copies within two years of publication, becoming 'a household book and a household phrase'.[24] For Seeley, the transformation of England into 'Greater

Britain' was the most momentous tendency in modern English history. Though it has been claimed that he was not a racist, and that in his discussion of Britain's responsibility for governing India 'there are no overtones of racial superiority',[25] Seeley himself gave the game away when he wrote that the British in India 'hold the position not merely of a ruling but of an educating and civilising race', that they were 'teachers and civilisers'.[26]

The racist tradition established by these giants towering over nineteenth-century British historiography – giants who, in Eric Williams's bitter but unanswerable phrase, 'betrayed scholarship and history'[27] – was carried on in the twentieth century by Hugh Egerton, Professor of Colonial History at Oxford. In his *British Colonial Policy in the XXth Century* (1922), Part II of which was entitled 'The Government of Backward Races', Egerton wrote that 'a justification for British imperialism' was 'to rescue the races of Africa from the servile status that had become engrained in their blood', and that 'to claim equality for the black man ... is to fly in the face of both science and instinct'.[28] From this it was only a short step to the popular Tory racism of a Sir Arthur Bryant, who wrote in his *English Saga* (1940) that, in Africa, Britain had within a single generation transformed 'provinces which for centuries had been savage areas of vice, fetishism, slavery, filth and pestilence'.[29]

Not surprisingly, the racism that tainted the central strand of the British historiographical tradition was specially virulent in those branches of the subject which treated of Caribbean, Indian, and African history. The reader of James Rodway's *History of British Guiana* (1891–94) was told that 'the negro ... troubles himself about nothing that may result from his actions unless it is impressed on him very strongly', so that, 'in dealing with tropical subject-races, a display of force is necessary and generally successful.'[30] The reader of A. Caldecott's *The Church in the West Indies* (1898) learnt that 'the Negro has not yet attained to the elevation of character necessary to sustain the higher order of family life'.[31] And the reader of W. P. Livingstone's *Black Jamaica* (1899) was assured that 'the black man ... on the eve of emancipation, was a child, ignorant, helpless, irresponsible. His mind was dark and stagnant, moving, if at all, to the blind impulses of superstition and fear'; moreover 'the advancement of the negro is contingent on his association with the white race', for 'without the stimulus of this factor he cannot better himself.'[32]

British historians of India were 'mostly influenced by the spirit of jingoism', writes the doyen of Indian historians, Ramesa Chandra Majumdar. He goes on:

> There was, besides, the over-powering sense of racial superiority which made even some eminent Englishmen, including Governors-General and British Cabinet ministers, look upon the Indians as little better than animals or primitive savages. It is therefore scarcely a matter of surprise that the British historians would give a picture of Indian history, during the British rule, which suffered to a very large degree from distortion and suppression of truth, biased judgment, and wrong inference, wherever the British prestige was likely to be damaged by a narration of actual events.[33]

To their credit, Edward Thompson and G. T. Garratt made a similar criticism in their *Rise and Fulfilment of British Rule in India* (1934). They complained that histories of British India had become less frank, full, and interesting in the previous 50 years, and that 'a constant silent censorship' had made British-Indian history 'the worst patch in current scholarship'.[34] And the attempts, from Mill onwards, 'to demonstrate that India was historically inferior to Europe ... indirectly served to justify British Indian imperialism'.[35]

As for African history, as recently as 1963 the then Regius Professor of Modern History at Oxford could dismiss it out of hand as the 'gyrations of barbaric peoples in insignificant corners of the globe'.[36] And, at a meeting of the Historical Association in January 1986, the Regius Professor of Modern History at Cambridge was hardly less scathing when he declared: 'We need more English history, and not this non-existent history of ethnic entities and women.'[37]

Children's Books

In his famous but now little-read study of *Imperialism* (1902), the economist J. A. Hobson complained about 'the persistent attempt to seize the school system for Imperialism masquerading as patriotism'. He added:

> To capture the childhood of the country ... to poison its early understanding of history by false ideals and pseudo-heroes ... to feed the always overweening pride of race ... to fasten this base insularity of mind and morals upon the little children of a nation and to call it patriotism is as foul an abuse of education as it is possible to conceive.[38]

Racism was in fact widely and persistently disseminated through school-books and other texts prepared for the education, or amusement, of children. The English history textbooks published between 1800 and 1914 have been studied by Valerie E. Chancellor, who finds that 'while Europeans were granted some respect, the peoples of Africa and Asia who came to form part of Britain's Empire were less kindly treated.' The most frequent impression conveyed about Indians is that they are 'cruel and totally unfitted to rule themselves'. The general opinion in textbooks was that the Indians were lucky to be under British rule. And 'much the same condescending and paternalistic attitude' was expressed towards Africans. The profitability of empire and its connection with the growth of British trade were hardly ever referred to, but there were plenty of descriptions of 'a noble national stereotype compared to inferior races'.[39] Here are three examples of how British schoolchildren were taught to see black people.

The first comes from Cassell's *Class History of England*, published in the second decade of free compulsory schooling. Girls and boys studying this textbook were told that, in the British Empire, 'we are face to face with barbarous peoples, whom it is profitless to conquer, yet amongst whom it is difficult otherwise to enforce peace and order'. This difficulty 'meets every nation which goes forth to carry civilisation amongst uncivilised peoples'.[40]

Twenty years later, black people were not only 'barbarous' and 'uncivilised' but also lazy, naked, and given to human sacrifice. A new generation of schoolchildren, reading Thomas Nelson's *The World and its People* (1903), learnt that:

> the negro is best described as an overgrown child, vain, self-indulgent, and fond of idleness, but 'with a good heart' ... Life is so easy to him in his native home that he has never developed the qualities of industry, self-denial, and forethought ... The negroes have never yet united in a strong and stable kingdom. He lives in a hut built of mud, reeds, or grasses, and wears little or no clothing ... Amongst the negro tribes wholesale human sacrifices are common.[41]

Our third example, published by the Clarendon Press in 1911, was the fruit of a collaboration between C. R. L. Fletcher and Rudyard Kipling. Their *School History of England* was designed for pupils under the age of 13. This simple and mendacious little book told them that the black inhabitants of the West Indies were:

> lazy, vicious and incapable of any serious improvement, or of work except under compulsion. In such a climate a few bananas will sustain the life of a negro quite sufficiently; why should he work to get more

than this? He is quite happy and quite useless, and spends any extra wages which he may earn upon finery.[42]

Significantly, school textbooks often quoted the classic nineteenth-century historians; indeed, Froude and Seeley 'maintained their grip upon school history teaching until after the Second World War'.[43] Nor can it be claimed that there has been much progress in this area since then. David Killingray's 1977 study of 'African history in the classroom' revealed that:

> For the majority of schools Africa's past is still either ignored, denigrated or distorted ... In many syllabuses Africa is a vast *tabula rasa* awaiting the appearance of the white man ... Africa is reduced to an anthropological zoo. It is not uncommon for teachers to illustrate lessons about *early man* by using film of *present day* hunting and gathering societies, a strategy which can lead children . . . to conclude that Africa is still in the stone age and that there is a hierarchy of mankind.[44]

In general, as Brian Street has pointed out, 'the concepts of Race and Social Evolution are still employed in the school book without the challenge that they are submitted to in the wider intellectual society.' Nor is it merely a question of how history and geography are taught. The teaching of English literature also deserves close scrutiny, since 'the literature used by teachers of English was often written at a time when other peoples were seen as "inferior" and debased'.[45]

Turning from school-books to the popular literature produced for children in the heyday of colonialism, we find the same crude racist message being rammed home again and again. Just as travel accounts caricatured black people as lazy, insolent and repellent; just as the new cheap newspapers of the 1890s were characterized by 'lack of any human appreciation of ... anything or anybody alien to English experience';[46] so the popular juvenile literature that poured from the presses at the turn of the century consistently portrayed black people as inferior. By 1880 more juvenile books were being published in Britain than any other type of literature, and over two dozen magazines, mostly directed to adolescent males, were appearing weekly on the news-stands. These usually sold for a penny, and the *Boy's Own Paper* claimed a circulation of over 1 million.[47]

In the widely circulated adventure stories of Frederick Marryat,

Thomas Mayne Reid, William H. G. Kingston, Robert M. Ballantyne, George A. Henty and William Stables, Africans are invariably described as ugly, animal-like, unintelligent, incompetent in abstract thought, physically dirty, cowardly, boastful, lazy, childish, and given to lying and thieving; African customs and behaviour are viewed as barbarous; African social and political organization is described as primitive.[48] With Henty in particular the political implications are made plain and simple: 'Easy domination of a native is a theme running through all the stories ... Submission is complete, service is total ... The servant ... is held in thrall by an Englishman's inherent superiority.'[49]

Patrick A. Duane, who has made a close study of the periodical literature produced for juveniles in Victorian times, finds that black people were ranged in a kind of 'racial preference hierarchy', with black Australians at the lower end of the scale. Descriptions of Africans – the 'typical negro' had a thick skull and a tiny brain – showed the extent to which 'scientific' racism was accepted and regurgitated, as was the notion that all black people looked alike: the *Boy's Own Paper* suggested in 1884 that they found it hard to distinguish among themselves. Duane sums up his findings as follows:

> Allowing for the particular biases of individual authors and the different tone of the periodicals, there was still a high degree of uniformity in the attitudes and stereotypes which were expressed in popular juvenile literature ... The black races were unanimously held as the most primitive of the world's peoples ... The gulf between black and white was too immense to ever be breached ...
>
> The Victorian youth who had avidly consumed the novels and periodicals of his period was not likely to change his attitudes when he ventured overseas. The young Briton who expected to meet, say, an ignorant and child-like African native invariably did so; natives who did not conform to their expected roles would be dismissed as unusual exceptions.[50]

The racist bias of the literature produced for children by British authors continued into the twentieth century; it still continues. Many of the 'classics' of children's literature, ancient and modern, are periodically reprinted with their objectionable features retained, and are still widely read.[51] Bob Dixon, for whom 'a particularly strong aspect of the indoctrination carried out in children's literature is that of racism', instances the Doctor Dolittle stories of Hugh Lofting and various works by Enid Blyton. Lofting illustrated his own books, and in text and illustrations alike he invariably portrayed black people as grotesque. In Blyton's *The Little Black Doll*, first published in 1937 and reissued in 1965, a doll's black face is a feared stigma which has to be removed before this doll can be accepted by the other toys. The black doll has to suffer, act as a servant, and undergo ritual purification by water. Once he has become pink instead of black, he is 'a nice-looking doll ... as good as any other', and thinks the toys will perhaps like him now he is 'no longer different'. Elsewhere in the Blyton corpus (*Here Comes Noddy Again*) the golliwog, 'a doll with crudely stylised racial characteristics which are African in type' – a doll habitually presented by this author in evil and menacing roles – becomes a serious threat to the hero, with whom the young reader or listener may be presumed to identify. A group of golliwogs, closely associated with fear and darkness, brutally steal Noddy's property. In one illustration they are shown tearing the clothes off his back. They then abandon him, naked, alone, and very frightened, in a dark wood. In Blyton's *Five Fall into Adventure* (1950) a young girl is terrified by 'a horrible, dreadful face': 'It had nasty, gleaming eyes, and it looked very dark – perhaps it was a black man's face!'[52]

Several generations of English children were brought up on this kind of nonsense, which is as hurtful to the young black reader as it is harmful to the young white reader.

Part III
Resistance

14
The Struggle against Slavery

Nowhere within the British Empire were black people passive victims. On the contrary, they were everywhere active resisters. Far from being docile, they resisted slavery and colonialism in every way open to them. Their resistance took many different forms, both individual and collective. It ranged from a watchful and waiting pretence of acceptance – a subtle if elementary form of individual resistance to slavery – right up to large-scale mass uprisings and national liberation movements.

On the African coast, resistance began before the slave-ships sailed. Slaves would try to make a dash for freedom at the very point of sale, and there were frequent uprisings, both by those locked up awaiting shipment[1] and by those already embarked.[2] Against all the odds, some of these desperate attempts succeeded.

Resistance continued in the living hell of the 'middle passage'. Incomplete records suggest that there was an actual uprising on perhaps no more than one slave voyage in ten. All the same,

> few voyages were ever completed without the discovery or threat of slave conspiracy, and no slaving captain throughout the history of the Atlantic trade ever sailed without a whole armory of guns and chains plus as many white crewmen as he could recruit and keep alive to act as seaborne jailers.[3]

Shipboard rebellions were sometimes made possible by the active help of the children who numbered anything up to one in five of the human cargoes. These children would get hold of knives, matchets, and other weapons and smuggle them to the men chained up in the holds.[4]

Throughout the Caribbean, as long as slavery lasted, resistance was the norm, not the exception. The slaves would do as little work as possible, a form of resistance interpreted by stupid or unimaginative observers as laziness. They would 'lose' and damage their working tools. They would feign illness, inflict injuries on themselves, sometimes kill themselves either individually or in groups – a cry, not of despair, but of defiance. Cultural resistance took the shape of songs and dances either blisteringly satirizing the planters and their families or else preparing the slaves for rebellion – as did, for instance, the kalinda of Dominica, Trinidad, and elsewhere, a stick-fighting dance that no doubt derives from African dances teaching young men the martial arts. Countless numbers of slaves resisted by running away; this became an increasingly common practice, so that in Jamaica, in the decade before emancipation, there were more runaways than ever before.[5] In revenge for acts of cruelty, slaves sometimes beat planters and overseers to death or poisoned them. The ever-present threat of rebellion cost the slaves less than actual revolt and kept the planters in a state of perpetual apprehension. But serious uprisings were far more frequent than historians have been prepared to acknowledge until quite recently.[6]

Michael Craton, in his illuminating book *Testing the Chains* (1982), lists no fewer that 75 slave rebellions in the British West Indies between the years 1638 and 1837 – roughly one every two-and-a-half years. All but 17 of these rebellions involved at least hundreds of slaves and 22 involved thousands or many thousands.[7] Orlando Patterson points out that during Jamaica's 180 years of slavery under British rule, 'hardly a decade went by without a serious, large-scale revolt threatening the entire system.'[8]

What Craton calls 'the first pamphlet ever to describe to readers in England the realities of slave unrest' appeared in London as early as 1676. It was a 14-page pamphlet giving news of a 'Conspiracy, which had like in one Moment to have defaced the most Flourishing Colony the *English* have in the World'.[9] This uprising in Barbados, the first large-scale slave rebellion in the British Caribbean, was led by 'an ancient Gold-Cost Negro' called Cuffee and 'a sturdy Rogue' called Tony. Martial law was declared and over 100 suspects were put on trial. Six were burnt alive; 11 were beheaded; another 25 were executed later; the rest were either deported, or restored to their owners after being savagely flogged.

Such repression did not prevent three further rebellions in Barbados over the next 17 years, in the first of which, in 1683, handwritten leaflets were distributed calling on the slaves to rise. These leaflets were written in English, already the lingua franca of Africans from different ethnic groups; one of them, preserved in the Public Record Office, is reproduced in Craton's book. It begins 'Brothers', and asserts that 'wee have most of all Countreyes of our Side' – i.e. that Africans of different ethnic groups were united in the struggle.[10]

Nine years later, in 1692, a plot extending over the whole island 'utterly shocked' the Barbados planters, for it was 'the most widespread and carefully planned to date'. Two of the leaders, Ben and Sambo, were seized during an audacious attempt to rescue a number of slaves arrested for 'disorderly conduct' and, after four days' starvation on the gibbet, Ben turned King's evidence. The conspirators, who included carpenters, bricklayers, wheelwrights, sawyers, blacksmiths, and grooms, had worked out a detailed plan of campaign, right down to organizing a slave army of nine regiments: six of infantry and three of cavalry.[11]

Between 1655 and 1740, the first 85 years of English occupation of Jamaica, the island was in a constant state of revolt. By the mid-1720s the maroons, or runaway slaves, numbered several thousands, and they were waging guerrilla warfare all over the island. £5 per head was paid for each maroon killed, on production of the ears to a justice of the peace; those captured alive were tortured and burnt to death.[12] But the maroons seemed invincible. One planter wrote in 1733: 'We are in terrible circumstances in respect to the rebellious Negroes. They get the better of all our partys, our men are quite dispirited and dare not look them in the face in the Open Ground or in Equal Numbers.'[13] Another wrote in the following year that the rebels 'openly appear in Arms and are daily Increasing'.[14] At length the British authorities were forced to sue for peace and bring this First Maroon War to an end by granting the rebels their freedom.

Contrary to the propaganda later put out by the planters, the peace negotiations were held with the undefeated guerrilla leader Cudjoe on ground of his own choosing and at the request of the British. A peace treaty consisting of 15 articles was signed on 1 March 1739. Its chief provisions were a guarantee to Cudjoe and his followers of a 'perfect state of freedom and liberty', and the establishment of what nowadays would be called a liberated area, 15,000 acres in extent, throughout which the maroons had the right to grow crops, raise stock, and hunt. Another band of maroons, led by Quao, signed a similar but rather less favourable treaty four months later, after winning a major victory over a force of several hundred soldiers and sailors.

A feature of both treaties was that, in order to gain their own freedom, the maroons undertook to perform policing duties against future runaways and rebels. And in fact Cudjoe and his followers helped to suppress later slave rebellions in 1742 and 1760–1.[15]

One of the outstanding leaders of the Jamaican maroons in the first half of the eighteenth century was the redoubtable Nanny, the woman who gave her name to Nanny Town in the Blue Mountains. Nanny, of Asante origin, was only one of a great many enslaved black women who played a heroic part in both passive and active resistance to slavery.

Because of her fortitude and intransigence – she repudiated Cudjoe's peace treaty and later accepted similar terms for her own people only with the greatest reluctance – Nanny is the most celebrated of these women freedom fighters. She was dreaded by the planters, and they thankfully rewarded the slave who murdered her.[16]

Antigua, in the Leeward Islands, was the scene of an island-wide slave plot in 1735–36. It was led by Tackey (otherwise known as Court), Tomboy, Scipio, Hercules, Jack, Ned, Fortune, Secundi, and Jacko: 'committed and able leaders, whose responsibilities included interpreting to their followers the signs of the whites' weakness or unpreparedness, convincing them of their own strength, and generally securing their active cooperation'.[17] The conspirators had been planning to blow up the governor and gentry during the annual ball commemorating the coronation of George II, then to seize forts and shipping. The ball was postponed, the plot was discovered, and three traitors informed on the leaders. As part of the preparations for the rising, Tackey and Tomboy had openly staged a 'Military dance and Shew' – in fact an Asante war dance (*Ikem*) – to find out how many followers they could count on; it had been attended by nearly 2,000 slaves. A few days later, a slave had shouted to a constable trying to disperse a crowd: 'Damn you boy its your turn now, but it will be mine by and by and soon too.' Ned, while in jail, was said to have told his imprisoned comrades 'to keep their minds to themselves and to be true to their Trust'. Of the 88 slaves executed for their part in the plot, 77 were burnt alive, 6 were starved to death on gibbets, and 5 were broken on the wheel.[18]

What Craton calls 'a convulsion of plantocratic shock' was produced by the Jamaican uprising of 1760–61, in which approximately 30,000 slaves took part.[19] The rebels seized muskets and gunpowder, burnt down a sugar factory, fired the canes, stormed and burnt the planters' great houses, and killed about 60 whites – though they spared the overseer of the Trinity estate, who had a reputation for 'singular tenderness and humanity'.[20] There was widespread panic and confusion among the planters, and it was 18 months before the rebellion was finally put down. Tacky, the young man who led it, was shot dead during a battle and his head was displayed on a pole in Spanish Town. Between 300 and 400 rebels were estimated to have been killed during the fighting or to have killed themselves rather than be captured. Few, if any, surrendered. Of those who were taken prisoner, 500 were transported, and 100 were executed in the usual barbaric fashion. One, hung to starve on a gibbet in the centre of Kingston, took nine days to die. Another, condemned to be burnt alive,

> was made to sit on the ground, and his body being chained to an iron stake, the fire was applied to his feet. He uttered not a groan, and saw his legs reduced to ashes with the utmost firmness and composure; after which, one of his arms by some means getting loose, he snatched a brand from the fire that was consuming him, and flung it in the face of the executioner.[21]

The slave plot discovered in Jamaica's Hanover parish in 1776, led by Sam, Charles, Caesar, and Prince, again deeply shocked the planters, since it drew in for the first time the locally born *elite* of drivers, craftsmen and domestic servants, who in the governor's words, had 'never before engaged in Rebellions'.[22] This was the first Caribbean slave uprising to follow the outbreak of the American Revolutionary War (1775–83), and there is no doubt that the rebels had it in mind to take advantage of British preoccupations elsewhere and, in particular, of the dispatch of troops from the Jamaican port of Lucea for the campaign in Florida. Seventeen slaves were put to death, 45 transported, and 11 severely flogged.[23]

In the 'almost ungovernable' island of Dominica, maroon resistance 'stretched back in an unbroken ... thread at least to the beginning of British colonization'[24] in 1761; and the period from 1785 to 1790 saw the island's First Maroon War. A dozen Dominican maroon leaders of the time are known to us by name: Congo Ray, Balla, Zombie, Jupiter, Juba, Cicero, Hall, Jacko, Coree Greg, Sandy and Pharcell (or Farcel).[25] No sooner had the governor announced to the Assembly that this emergency was over than a new movement was afoot, with the slaves putting forward a novel claim. For the first time in the British Caribbean, they demanded freedom to work for themselves on two, three, or four days in the week. And when this demand was rejected they refused to work at all. This 'proto-industrial action', as Craton terms it, was merely the prelude to a new uprising. 'Notions and opinions', wrote the governor, 'have certainly got root in the minds of the slaves in general, which I much apprehend will militate against their ever again being such faithful, obedient and contented servants as they were formerly.'[26] Unrest continued, with a bloodily suppressed mutiny by the 600 black troops of the Eighth West India Regiment at Prince Rupert's Bay in 1802.[27]

Radical 'notions and opinions' were not confined to Dominica. By 1795, when a major uprising on Grenada drew in most of the island's slaves, news had spread throughout the Caribbean both of the French Revolution and – a message of hope and deliverance from much closer at hand – the Haitian Revolution that had begun in 1791. Encouraged and inspired by the struggle of their fellow-slaves in Haiti, which had sent a 'shudder of terror' through the British plantocracy,[28] more than 7,000 slaves paralysed Grenada for nearly two years under the leadership of Julien Fédon. The slaves had sent to Guadeloupe two delegates who returned early in 1795 as captains in the French revolutionary army, bringing with them arms, ammunition, tricolour cockades, caps of liberty, and a battle flag that bore the slogan *Liberté, égalité ou la Mort*. The uprising, a few days later, took the whites utterly by surprise, and before long the governor himself, Ninian Home, was in the hands of the insurgents. A British officer, Colin Lindsay, sent from Martinique with 150 regular soldiers to put down the rising, shot himself when his strategy failed. Massive reinforcements poured in from Barbados and Martinique, but their efforts were no more successful. 'To all intents and purposes', writes Craton, 'at the beginning of 1796 Grenada was a black republic under arms, with St George's the single imperial enclave.'[29] The freedom fighters, who had set up their own revolutionary administration, were defeated only when they were outnumbered ten to one – and even then Grenada was peaceful only on the surface. 'The effects of Fédon's rebellion were never fully mended ... Large plantations were never fully re-established and never flourished as did those in newly acquired Trinidad or Guyana.'[30] Fédon himself was never captured – at one point he escaped by diving over a precipice into a clump of brushwood, with his pursuers only three yards behind him – and he became a legendary hero.[31]

Ideas stemming from the French and Haitian revolutions were prominent also in the 1796–97 uprising in St Lucia: the so-called Brigands' War. Many slaves went into battle, many to the scaffold, crying '*Vive la république!*' The insurgents' scorched-earth tactics made it hard to feed the soldiers who hunted them, and for the British this was 'a deeply disturbing campaign, like damming water with sand'. The British commander, General John Moore, had a narrow escape when the boat he was in was pursued by rebels in canoes. One of his regiments, the Thirty-first, lost 22 officers and 841 other ranks within a year. Moore's successor, Colonel James Drummond, brought the war to an end by offering terms that the rebels found acceptable.[32]

Between 1809 and 1814 Dominica was again the scene of continuous fighting, the island's Second Maroon War. The maroons, estimated to number at least 800, were led by Quashie, Elephant, Soleil, Battre Bois, Hill, Nicholas, Diano, Noel, Robin, Apollo, Jean Zombi, Lewis, Moco, Nico, and Jacko. The last of these, it was said, lived in the forest as a guerrilla for over 40 years. The governor, George Ainslie, put a price on Quashie's head, whereupon Quashie immediately offered $2,000 for the governor's head. The savage fighting came to an end only after two hurricanes, in 1813, had devastated the maroons' provision grounds in the mountains.[33]

The 1816 slave revolt in Barbados was led by Bussa, Jackey, King Wiltshire, Dick Bailey, Johnny Cooper, and a literate, militant, and highly articulate woman slave called Nanny Grigg, who told her fellow-slaves that the only way to get freedom was to fight for it, 'otherwise they would not get it; and the way they were to do, was to set fire, as that was the way they did in Saint Domingo [Haiti]'. Six hours after the first fires had been lit, the revolt had spread to 70 of the largest estates. The authorities suppressed it with great cruelty and bloodshed, burning countless slave houses and unleashing the hated militia to kill men, women and children indiscriminately. Seventy rebels were summarily executed in the field and a further 144 were put to death later. The Speaker of the Barbadian Assembly declared afterwards: 'The Insurrection has been quelled, but the spirit is not subdued, nor will it ever be subdued whilst these dangerous doctrines which have been spread abroad continue to be propagated among the Slaves.'[34]

In 1823 about 12,000 slaves rose in revolt on the east coast of Demerara, one of the three Guyana colonies the British had finally taken from the Dutch 20 years before. There was in the Guyana colonies a long tradition of slave rebellions, suppressed with the utmost ferocity, and in 1763 slaves led by Africans had controlled the entire colony of Berbice for over a year. In 1795 Demerara itself, under Dutch rule, had witnessed a large-scale revolt, partly stirred up by the remarkable agitation of a woman of mixed parentage named Nancy Wood. The 1823 insurgents, who demanded unconditional emancipation, were led by a chapel deacon called Quamina and his son Jack Gladstone. In a half-hour parley with the governor at the start of the rebellion, a group of armed slaves listened coldly to his expostulations and retorted that 'God had made them of the same flesh and blood as the whites, that they were tired of being Slaves to them.' But the rebels were pitifully armed for the task they had set themselves, for they had between them fewer than 100 muskets besides cutlasses and home-made pikes. Not surprisingly, they were slaughtered by the regulars and militia, who dispersed them within minutes. At least 23 were shot after drumhead courts martial, and their bodies were hung to rot outside their houses. The elderly Quamina was tracked down and shot dead, and his body was hung in chains at the front of the Success plantation, owned by John Gladstone, father of a future British prime minister. Martial law continued for five months, with crude show trials and public executions;

at least 12 of the rebels were decapitated, the heads being displayed on poles. After a trial lasting 28 days, the Reverend John Smith, a British missionary, was found guilty of complicity with the rebels and sentenced to be hanged. He died of tuberculosis after six months' detention; a reprieve signed by George IV arrived in the colony a week later. Soon afterwards John Gladstone was declaring that philanthropy was misplaced and Christianity dangerous in relation to slaves whose only ambition was to live in indolence. And the governor of Demerara was writing: 'The spirit of discontent is anything but extinct, it is alive as it were under its ashes, and the Negro mind although giving forth no marked indications of mischief to those not accustomed to observe it, is still agitated, jealous and suspicious.'[35]

The year 1823 also saw a slave uprising, the so-called Argyle War, in the St George's, St Mary's, and Hanover parishes of Jamaica. Crops were burnt, 11 rebels were hanged, and many others were flogged or transported.[36] From then on – partly under the impact of the anti-slavery agitation in Britain – the whole Caribbean was simmering with discontent. There were outbreaks in Tortola, one of the Virgin Islands (1823, 1830, and 1831); the Bahamas (1830, led by a slave called Pompey); and Antigua, where slaves from many estates marched on the capital in 1831 to protest against the abolition of Sunday markets, winning the concession of an extra free day.[37]

The climax of this massive upsurge of discontent in the British West Indies - an upsurge fuelled by rumours of emancipation as well as by the circulation of revolutionary ideas – was the mass uprising that gripped western Jamaica in 1831–32. A network of religious meetings that had developed around the mission churches served as a ready-made structure within which the slaves could organize; so the 1831–32 rebellion has come to be known as the Baptist War. This was the greatest rebellion in Jamaican history. Under the charismatic leadership of Samuel 'Daddy' Sharpe, it mobilized 60,000 slaves over an area of 750 square miles; and it was undoubtedly one of the main factors that led to the abolition of slavery in 1833.

It is not hard to account for the remarkable strength of this uprising. The island had suffered a six-month drought followed by heavy rains, and the harvesting of provisions had been seriously affected. Smallpox and dysentery were widespread. The planters had been holding a series of public protest meetings against the anti-slavery campaign in Britain. Some had openly advocated armed revolt; some had spoken of seceding from the British Empire; and the possibility of getting help from the United States had been openly discussed. In November 1831 the Assembly had refused to discuss a proposal to abolish the flogging of women slaves, prohibited eight years before by an Order in Council. Jamaican slaves were convinced that the planters were conspiring to deprive them of freedom that was either imminent or, as some supposed, had already been granted:

> Every one was talking of the proceedings of the British parliament; every one said that the king of England was going to give freedom to the slaves; and every one [among the planters] indulged himself in the unrestrained expression of his anger ... The master of one slave told him 'that freedom was come from England, but that he would shoot every d---d black rascal before he should get it'. Another heard his master say, 'the king is going to give us free, but he hoped all his friends will be of his mind, and spill their blood first'.[38]

The rebels' political awareness had been developed in the missions to a large extent: 'The slaves took up the Christian message, blended it with their traditional religion, and forged a moral case for action on behalf of their own freedom.'[39] But their fighting organizations had been built by leaders who were independent of the missions and who 'directed the widespread excitement and discontent into action, utilizing religious meetings and the authority of the missionaries to promote the cause of freedom'.[40] Thus Samuel Sharpe, Baptist convert and fluent orator, whose reading of the Bible had convinced him that the slaves were entitled to freedom, built up an independent network whose initial aim was a mass strike throughout the St James and Trelawney parishes. The strikers would not use force unless attacked, in which case they would set fire to the big houses but not to canes and factories. But this passive resistance was to be backed by an armed revolt. About 150 slaves with 50 guns formed a 'Black Regiment' commanded by Johnson, Campbell (a carpenter), Robert Gardner (a head wagoner), and Thomas Dove. Johnson and Campbell were appointed colonels; Gardner and Dove, captains. Other slaves were organized into companies, each responsible for guarding its estate boundaries and sending intelligence reports to regimental headquarters on the Greenwich estate, on the boundary of Hanover and Westmoreland parishes.

A minor incident sparked off the rising. A lawyer struck a woman slave for allegedly stealing canes, and two constables sent to make arrests were disarmed and beaten. Then, on the evening of 27 December 1831, the firing of the trash house on the Kensington estate signalled the start of the rebellion. Beacons soon dotted the mountains for miles. 'The rebels had chosen their beacon points for maximum effect on whites and slaves alike', writes Craton.[41] Messengers ran from estate to estate shouting: 'No watchman now! Nigger man, burn the house – burn buckra house! Brimstone come! Bring fire and burn massa house!' Next day the Black Regiment fought and defeated the Western Interior militia, which had retreated from its barracks, and forced its further retreat to Montego Bay. Within a week the insurgents controlled the whole western interior of Jamaica and had cut off all communications across the island. White women and children were hastily embarked in ships anchored in Montego Bay.

Though they had been successful against the militia, the rebel forces could not hold their own against British regulars. They lacked military experience and guerrilla skills, and the back of the armed rebellion was soon broken. What followed was a war of attrition, in which slave houses and provision grounds were destroyed and about 200 slaves were killed. Among these was Patrick Ellis who, surrounded, refused to surrender and, presenting his breast to the advancing troops, cried: 'I am ready; give me your volley. Fire, for I will never again be a slave.'[42]

Meanwhile the strike was broken piecemeal by intimidation. On the Georgia estate in Trelawney parish, for instance, the slaves' village was attacked at dawn. When the strikers sat tight and refused to leave they were dragged out one by one, and one man was shot as an example. Individual acts of defiance are recorded: one woman put down her washing at the water tank to toss a fire stick into the trash house as the militia approached the estate. The militia displayed an appetite for revenge. On one Trelawney estate, where all the slaves had been pardoned by the British commander-in-chief in person, a militia detachment commanded by the estate's attorney turned up an hour later, and the attorney ordered a slave to be shot.

In formal courts martial, 427 slaves were tried, of whom 232 were executed. An unknown number were tried by illicit drumhead courts martial, with neither defence procedure nor ratification of sentences. Those condemned by either type of court martial 'were often executed almost before the ink on the court record was dry – if, indeed, a proper record was kept at all'.[43] Prisoners were put to death for the most trivial offences: one for cooking one of the estate hogs; another for hamstringing a cow and snapping a gun five times. A further 200 slaves were tried by civil courts, and 130 of these were executed. The total of 627 indicted came from nearly 250 estates. A large majority were field slaves, but there were also 39 drivers, 35 headmen of other types, 48 carpenters, 10 coopers, 10 masons and 9 blacksmiths. About one in five had been born in Africa. None was under 20, and few were under 25. The oldest was a 70-year-old African. Seventy-five of those indicted were women, but only two of those were executed. Most of the women were sentenced to be flogged, like Elizabeth Ball, a free black woman from Montego Bay, who was sentenced to 24 lashes and six months in prison for sedition. A few white people who took the side of the rebels were also brought to trial: John Ellery, a sailor, was sent to jail for 14 days; Alfred Smith, an estate bookkeeper, and the Reverend Henry Pfeiffer, a Moravian missionary, were acquitted, as were several others.[43]

Many of the rebels went to their deaths with great heroism. A Methodist missionary, the Reverend Henry Bleby, wrote in his *Death Struggles of Slavery* (1853):

> I have seen many led out to die, who were as calm and undismayed in walking to the scaffold as if they had been proceeding to their daily toil ... With the dignified bearing of men untroubled with misgivings as to the justice of their cause, they yielded themselves to their doom.

Bleby visited Samuel Sharpe several times in the condemned cell and found him 'certainly the most intelligent and remarkable slave I ever met with'. Sharpe told Bleby: 'I would rather die upon yonder gallows than live in slavery.' Dressed in a new white suit, he marched to those gallows with a firm, dignified step, the last British slave to be executed before emancipation.[44]

But emancipation, when it came two years later, merely replaced the old slavery by a modified form called apprenticeship. For four years, as we have seen in Part I, the slaves had to perform 45 hours of unpaid labour per week. And there was resistance to this modified form of slavery, ranging from general 'unrest' to riots that have been strangely neglected by historians. On the island of St Kitts the resistance to apprenticeship was well organized, and the workers who took part demanded the right to wages in payment for their labour. As emancipation drew near the slaves were saying that 'they would give their souls to hell and their bodies to the sharks' rather than be bound to work as apprentices. Their slogan, as on many other islands, was: 'Me free; no bind; no work.' On the last day of slavery the slaves threw down their hoes and other tools and expressed their determination not to use them again. On the first day of apprenticeship almost all the St Kitts estates were totally or largely strike-bound. Some 'ringleaders' were flogged, but to no avail. The majority of the workers trooped off to the mountains, leaving fields and cattle untended. Martial law was proclaimed. Absentees' houses were burnt down and troops flushed them out by making a coordinated military advance into the mountains from both sides of the island. In the end the workers gave in and went back to the estates, remaining 'sulky', 'insolent' and 'provoking' to their 'superiors'. Sixteen, including two women, were tried for sedition, mutiny, and incitement. Five were banished to Bermuda; the others were flogged and imprisoned for various periods.[45]

This survey of the major slave revolts in the British Caribbean shows how absurd is the official myth that 'the ... Negro population, during the centuries of slavery, had little to do, save indirectly, with the shaping of events'.[46] Far from being the inert, passive victims that this persistent myth portrays, the slaves tied down large numbers of British troops in costly and demoralizing operations; caused endless trouble to planters and colonial governors; levied a huge tax on the plantation economy, in terms of crops and equipment destroyed; and made a massive cumulative contribution to emancipation. Yet if we judge the slave revolts strictly in terms of seizing and holding power – and, before the pivotal Haitian Revolution, this may well be an anachronistic criterion – they were unsuccessful. For their lack of success there were clear geographical, military and political reasons.

Except for British Honduras and the Guyana colonies, all Britain's possessions in the area were islands. Before the emergence of modern methods of transport and communication it was out of the question to coordinate resistance into a single powerful movement. Before the Haitian Revolution, the most the slaves could hope to achieve on any single island was protracted guerrilla warfare, for which the terrain of the interior of most of the islands was highly suitable. From the maroons' point of view, this was a survival strategy, not a strategy for taking power. The maroons were supreme realists, who neither demanded nor envisaged general emancipation or control of a whole colony. They showed their ruthless realism above all by signing peace treaties with the British. The latter, too, often showed themselves to be realistic – in that, by coming to terms with the maroons and using them as a kind of auxiliary police force against the rest of the slaves, they were applying their favourite strategy of divide and rule.

The Haitian Revolution came at a time when the occupying power, France, was in the throes of a massive social upheaval. The European chain binding the Caribbean snapped at its weakest link. The democratic ideas of the French Revolution – that all human beings had a natural right to liberty, equality, and the pursuit of happiness – gripped the Haitian masses. The Haitians unleashed the greatest slave revolt in human history and provided a powerful example to the nascent working-class movement in Europe of what could be achieved by organization, determination and *élan*. No favourable conjuncture in

Britain helped the British-held slaves in the Caribbean to settle accounts with their masters. All the same, as we have seen, they asserted their humanity and fighting spirit in every possible way and on every possible occasion. Over a period of almost 200 years they proved themselves to be 'the most dynamic and powerful social force in the colonies'.[47] And their unending resistance was the most important single factor in their emancipation.

15
The Caribbean after Emancipation

In all of Britain's Caribbean colonies, writes Michael Craton,

> the newly freed were continually harassed by the extension of British police, vagrancy, and masters and servants laws, applied by justices of the peace who were usually planters or by stipendiary magistrates strongly under plantocratic influence. The freedmen's ambitions to be peasant freeholders were hampered by relatively high prices for land, taxes that grossly favored the large landowners, and the enforcement of laws against squatting. Political expression was stifled, and where there were elections the franchise was denied to the black masses by loaded property qualifications. Though they could not control the larger economy, the colonial whites also made sure that they remained a local oligarchy, controlling all wholesale and most retail trade and obtaining legislation against the former slaves' informal marketing networks ... Those sugar plantations that survived became even more exploitative and impersonal through the inevitable quest for economies of scale ... Most blacks were ... employed casually, only when needed, at the most onerous and unpopular tasks ...
>
> When the emancipated slaves found their plight as miserable as in slavery days and their aspirations thwarted by their former owners, discontent mounted.[1]

Frank Cundall, in his *Political and Social Disturbances in the West Indies* (1906), lists 21 expressions of this discontent in the years between 1841 and 1905: 6 in Jamaica, 5 in British Guiana, 4 in Trinidad, 2 in Dominica, and one each in Barbados, British Honduras, Montserrat, and St Kitts.[2] The most important of these were the 1865 Morant Bay rebellion in Jamaica, the 1876 riots in Barbados, the 1903 'water riots' in Trinidad, and the riots of 1905 in British Guiana.

Though 'scarcely noted in most British histories',[3] Jamaica's 1865 rebellion, led by a peasant smallholder and local Baptist preacher called Paul Bogle, was the most serious – and most bloodily repressed – of all nineteenth-century expressions of discontent in the British Caribbean. It started at a time of drought and rising prices. A group of land-hungry peasants in St Ann parish, on the north coast of the island, petitioned Queen Victoria asking for some of 'Her Land' for them to cultivate on a cooperative basis. Her Majesty replied that the only solution to their problems lay in their working for wages 'steadily and continuously, at the times when their labour is wanted, and for so long as it is wanted'. Their salvation lay in 'their own industry and prudence', and not in 'any such schemes as have been suggested to them'.[4] In fact, of course, the great majority of Jamaicans were not wage-workers, but worked on their own land or on rented land. And it was simply not true that jobs were available. The reply to their petition, as callous as it was inappropriate, was inspired by Governor Edward Eyre, whose experience with subject peoples in Australia, New Zealand, and Trinidad had led him to the view that Jamaicans must be ruled with a rod of iron. And he caused 50,000 posters with the text of the reply to be stuck up all over the island, under the heading 'The Queen's Advice'.

Feelings, already running high, rose higher still when George William Gordon, a planter of mixed parentage, was sacked as vestryman and justice of the peace for venturing to criticize the way justice was operated in St Thomas's parish. Petitioners against his dismissal tramped 45 miles to see the governor, but he refused to receive them. Then a man whom police were trying to arrest for an alleged breach of the peace was rescued from the Morant Bay courthouse by a group of Paul Bogle's supporters. Warrants were issued for the arrest of Bogle and 27 of his followers, and when police went to the village of Stony Gut to arrest them they were driven back by the people. Next day several hundred men, armed with sticks, cutlasses, and five shotguns, marched on Morant Bay. After a few stones had been thrown the marchers were fired on by the militia, and seven were killed. The rebels burnt down the courthouse and several other buildings; killed a black magistrate and 18 white people (magistrates, militiamen and planters); and released 51 prisoners from the local jail.

Governor Eyre proclaimed martial law, put down the rising with the utmost severity, and took a most brutal and horrible revenge. British soldiers and sailors went on the rampage. A total of 439 people were shot down or executed. Six hundred, including women, were flogged with the utmost barbarity. Bogle was hanged from the yard-arm of a British ship. Gordon, after a hasty and ill-constituted court martial that heard totally inadequate evidence, was hanged in front of the burnt-out

Morant Bay courthouse. More than 1,000 houses were wantonly destroyed. 'Ah! my man!' said a captain of the Kingston Volunteers to one of his prisoners, 'we shall take a thousand of your black men's hearts for one white man's ear.'[5]

The month-long reign of terror caused an outcry in Britain. Eyre was turned into a Tory hero, but a Royal Commission found that excessive punishments had been inflicted. One result of the rebellion was the dissolution of the Jamaican Assembly, the island becoming a Crown Colony under direct Colonial Office rule.[6]

Following a proposal for a federation of the Windward Islands, strongly resisted by the planters, there were widespread disturbances in Barbados in 1876. After a man had been shot at a meeting on the Mount Prospect estate, in the parish of St Peter, a general uprising began. It was led by two brothers named Dottin, one of whom is described as waving a red flag, the other a sword. About 1,000 rebels roamed the island in well-organized groups, burning the planters' canes and killing their cattle. Meanwhile panic reigned in Bridgetown. The governor mobilized the troops, swore in 500 special constables, and succeeded in crushing the uprising in six days. Eight black people were killed and 30 wounded; 90 were sentenced for looting and arson. Barbados went on smouldering for many months.[7]

The 1903 riots in Trinidad followed a new waterworks ordinance intended to curtail the use of water in Port of Spain. The governor's decision that the public would not be admitted to a Council debate on this subject sparked off fierce fighting. The governor's carriage was wrecked and a block of government buildings known as the Red House was burnt to the ground. British sailors were landed, and there was a contest between bottles and stones from one side, bullets from the other. Sixteen people were killed – some shot, others brutally bayoneted – and 43 were injured.[8]

With the 1905 riots in British Guiana we come to a new period, when the industrial working class has emerged and entered the arena as an independent force with its own demands; eventually this class would become the backbone of the anti-colonialist struggle in the British West Indies.

The root cause of the 1905 events in British Guiana was the atrocious pay and conditions of the Guyanese workers. First to take action were Georgetown's casual dock labourers, who went on strike for higher wages. Soon the movement spread to neighbouring sugar estates, where it embraced sugar boilers, porters and stokers. A large number of people took to the streets. Police opened fire on crowds near the Ruimveldt factory, four of whose workers were badly injured and later died. The sight of four wounded workers being taken to hospital in a cart did not strike fear into people's hearts, as the authorities seem to have hoped it would, but served rather to inflame them. The news spread rapidly and, in the words of one newspaper report, 'three-fourths of the population of Georgetown seemed to have gone stark staring mad'. Though the Riot Act had been read, thousands surged through the streets and a crowd invaded the Public Buildings, forcing the governor to hide ignominiously behind closed doors. A group of women attacked a police station. Showered with stones and bottles, police patrols retaliated with rifle fire. Seven people, one of them a woman, were killed, and 17 badly wounded. Two British warships arrived, whose sailors were used to arrest alleged ringleaders. Sentences imposed on the 87 people convicted included six months' imprisonment and flogging for men; some women were ordered to have their heads shaved. The strike movement in British Guiana collapsed because the workers were not organized – embryonic working-class organizations set up in the late 1880s had not survived, and a British Guiana Labour Union was not formed until 1919. The strikers had no strike funds and were unable to hold out for long.[9]

Trinidad, where retail prices rose by 145 per cent between 1914 and 1919, witnessed a wave of strikes and mass struggle towards the end of the First World War and immediately afterwards. The movement began with a strike of oil and asphalt workers in 1917. Troops were called in and five of the leaders were thrown in jail. In the following year the Trinidad Workingmen's Association, representing skilled urban workers of African descent, was revitalized as a body offering leadership to the whole of the colony's working class. Unrest grew with the return home of Trinidadian ex-servicemen who had been disgracefully treated by the military authorities. Some of them, while stationed in Italy, had mutinied and then formed a secret Caribbean League advocating self-government for black people and strike action for higher wages after demobilization. As soon as they got back to Trinidad in 1919, the ex-servicemen set up the Returned Soldiers and Sailors Council and Organization, which staged public meetings at which they aired their grievances.

The same year saw a strike wave embracing Trinidad's dockers, railway workers, tramway workers, local authority employees, and asphalt workers. This strike movement developed into a serious challenge to British colonialism. In a telegram to the colonial secretary, the governor admitted that the populace had forced businesses to close and had stopped traffic in Port of Spain's business and administrative district; that the Inspector General of Constabulary had admitted that he could no longer ensure the town's safety unless concessions were made to the strikers; and that the authorities were afraid to open fire on rioters in case there were reprisals against white people living in country districts. Under pressure from the governor, the shipping agents conceded a 25 per cent wage increase to the dockers – a concession which had the effect of generating a fresh wave of strikes throughout the colony. Unrest spread to the neighbouring island of Tobago, where estate workers downed tools and marched through the streets of Scarborough. Police fired on a crowd attacking the government radio station, and a worker named Nathaniel Williams was shot dead. British marines were landed in Tobago to restore order. Early in 1920, the government arrested 99 Trinidadian workers' leaders and imprisoned 82 of them, including the dockers' leader James Braithwaite.[10]

Immediately after the First World War there was unrest also in British Honduras, Jamaica, Grenada and elsewhere in the British West Indies. But these events were merely the prelude to a revolutionary upsurge throughout the entire area in the 1930s. The movement presented such a formidable challenge to British rule that 'every British Governor called for warships, marines and aeroplanes', and 46 people were killed, 429 wounded, and thousands imprisoned.[11]

This new stage in the national liberation struggle began in the mainland colony of British Honduras. Here, in the 1930s, a large proportion of the population lived in great distress, which had been heightened by the hurricane of September 1931. There was high unemployment; those in work earned miserable wages; and many people were in debt to the Hurricane Loan Board. On 1 October 1934, the working class of British Honduras began a revolt against the colonial government. They were led by Antonio Soberanis Gomez, leader of the Labour and Unemployed Association, who is regarded as the father of Belizean nationalism. For months Gomez and his supporters had been campaigning for relief for the unemployed or work with a fair wage. Matters came to a head when a crowd of 500 occupied Belize Town's biggest sawmill, thus shutting down the colony's main employer. Then thousands of people raided a coconut warehouse, a timber yard, and the Public Works Department yard. The rebels fought a pitched battle with the police, who fired into the unarmed crowds and wounded a demonstrator named Absolem Pollard. The acting governor, in whose view the working class of the colony were 'riff-raff', was forced to promise $3,000 for immediate outdoor relief. One arrested worker received three years' hard labour, another two years, a third six months. Gomez himself was kept in jail for five weeks. In April 1935, helped by a woman called Euginia ('Ginger') Stanford or Staniford, he organized at Dangriga a strike of ill-paid government labourers, who fought back against the police that arrived to disperse their pickets. The Legislative Council then rushed through a drastic piece of legislation making virtually any criticism of the government a seditious act.[12]

In Trinidad, about 15,000 sugar workers went on strike in July 1934. 'Desperate men close to starvation', they attacked overseers, managers and policemen and set company buildings on fire.[13] In the following March it was the Trinidadian oil workers' turn to take to the streets, in protest against low wages, long hours, poor conditions, and fines for lateness. Later the same year came a series of strikes in British Guiana; an upheaval in St Vincent when the government decided to raise Customs duties; and a coal strike in St Lucia which led to the proclamation of a state of emergency, the mobilization of the local militia, and the landing of marines from a British warship. The year 1935 also witnessed a strike movement in the poverty-stricken island of St Kitts, where striking sugar workers were fired on by police; three workers were killed and eight wounded.

Fascist Italy's invasion of Ethiopia in 1935 greatly stimulated the national liberation movement throughout the Caribbean. Trinidad's dockers refused to unload Italian ships, and there was a marked surge of black consciousness and political awareness both there and in other British-held islands. But the root cause of the great strike movement that gripped Trinidad in June 1937 was the worsening living conditions of the masses: unemployment and underemployment, desperate poverty, malnutrition, deficiency diseases and atrocious housing. Despite the vast profits reaped by their British employers, Trinidadian oil workers were earning less than in the previous decade. Between 1935 and 1937 they were organized: in the south, by the Grenada-born labour leader Uriah Butler, who said he was conducting 'a heroic struggle for British justice for British Blacks in a British country'; in the north, by the socialist and anti-imperialist Negro Welfare, Cultural and Social Association (NWA), led by Jim Barrat, Elma François, Rupert Gittens, Christina King, Clement Payne and Bertie Perceval. The NWA also had strong support among the unemployed. When the Forest Reserve oil workers struck on 18 June 1937 there was an attempt to arrest Uriah Butler, who went into hiding, later gave himself up, and was tried and sentenced to two months' hard labour. The workers answered this attack on their leader with widespread strikes and rioting, and within 48 hours the strike was general. Two policemen were killed at Fyzabad; the police killed 12 workers and wounded 50. 'The rioting', writes Bridget Brereton, 'expressed the pent-up grievances and resentments of workers whose economic situation had deteriorated over the preceding years and who had no legitimate channels for the peaceful resolution of industrial problems.' The governor responded at first with certain concessions. But the oil companies put pressure on the Colonial Office, and the governor capitulated, switching suddenly from conciliation to repression and calling in British troops. One of the main results of the 1937 outbreak in Trinidad was the development of an organized trade union movement – though under Colonial Office and British Trades Union Congress tutelage, and with leaders who for the most part knuckled under to British paternalism.[14]

Fourteen people were killed and 47 injured when police fired 800 rounds of ammunition into unarmed crowds demonstrating in the Barbados capital of Bridgetown in July 1937. Over 500 were arrested, and some of these were sent to prison for five years, others for ten – sentences later reduced by the Colonial Secretary. The demonstrators were protesting against the arrest of a young Trinidad-born black activist called Clement Osbourne Payne, a friend of Uriah Butler and a member of the Trinidad Youth League. It was Payne who distributed the first-ever May Day pamphlets in Barbados. When he held 17 meetings at which he urged the workers to organize to improve their conditions, he soon had the police after him. People said: 'Because he opening we eyes they are trying to lock him up.' Arrested after leading a march on Government House, Payne was deported. This brought large numbers of people on the streets, damaging vehicles, pushing them into the sea, and breaking shop windows. With showers of bottles and stones the demonstrators chased the police into the central police station, from which they emerged armed with .303 rifles. Lightermen and stevedores went on strike, and the rising spread rapidly to rural districts, where poor and hungry people broke into shops and raided sweet-potato fields. Even the highly biased report of the commission of inquiry (the Deane Commission) admitted that hunger had helped to cause these outbreaks in country districts. In their view, said the commissioners, 'there was a large accumulation of explosive matter in the island to which the Payne incident only served as a detonator', adding that it was 'a question of undoubted stark poverty'. Four of Payne's supporters, Fitz Archibald ('Menzies') Chase, Mortimer ('Mortie') Skeete, Darnley ('Brain') Alleyne, and Ulric Grant, were beaten up unmercifully while in police custody, and their ordeal was the subject of songs handed down in the oral tradition. Chase was imprisoned for nine months for having 'incited' the crowd to riot merely by declaring: 'Tonight will be a funny day.' One result of the rising was the formation in 1938 of the Barbados Progressive League – popularly known as the 'First Party of the Barefoot

Man' – under the leadership of C. A. ('Chrissie') Brathwaite and Grantley Adams.[15]

In Jamaica, Britain's largest Caribbean colony, there had been sporadic unrest for several years. This unrest culminated in the great rebellion that lasted from April to June 1938. Jamaican workers and peasants downed tools, marched in demonstrations, looted shops, cut telephone wires, put up road-blocks, destroyed bridges, burnt crops, besieged the rich in their houses, and, armed only with sticks and stones, fought back against armed police patrols and troops. It was officially admitted that crowds were fired on 13 times between 23 May and mid-June. Twelve people were killed and 171 injured. 'In mid-1938 the Jamaican people made their own history', writes Ken Post. 'They shook the whole colonial system so severely that it was never quite the same again.'

The rising began with rioting and a strike at the Frome Estate in Westmoreland parish. More than 100 armed police were rushed in, and they killed four people of whom two were women, one elderly, the other pregnant. In retaliation the strikers set fire to the cane fields. Kingston dockers, public service workers, and tramway workers came out on strike, and thousands marched through the city centre, only to have their demonstration broken up by police wielding batons. The strikers fought back with stones and threw up barricades. They smashed street lamps to hamper night patrols. They overturned rubbish bins and set buildings on fire. Troops were brought in, and shot dead a woman and her young son. But when Kingston had been subdued the revolt spread to the rest of the island. In Spanish Town the sanitary workers stopped work and there was soon a general strike. The Montego Bay dockers, when they heard the news from Kingston, came out on strike and staged a hunger march. The railway workers soon joined in. There was a series of 'rolling strikes' as sugar and banana workers marched from estate to estate to spread the movement. Everywhere there were fierce clashes with police and troops. Four people were killed in the small town of Islington, in St Mary parish. Here, when police arrived and started confiscating the sticks some people were carrying, a man called Edgar Daley refused, declaring: 'No, not a raas. You have you gun. I have my stick.' He was bayoneted and his back was broken with rifle butts. In Trelawney a seaplane from the Royal Navy cruiser *Ajax* dispersed crowds outside a sugar factory by diving at them. Of the 480 people convicted afterwards, two, S. Kerr Coombs and H. C. Buchanan, were imprisoned for six months after they had exposed police brutality in St James.[16]

In Jamaica, as in Trinidad and Barbados, the rebellion led to the emergence of a substantial trade union movement. Another direct result of the wave of labour revolts was the appointment of the Moyne Commission to investigate conditions in the British West Indies (see pp. 30–2 above). In Jamaica the 1938 struggle also achieved, six years later, a long-overdue constitutional reform, with universal adult suffrage and an elected lower house.

The Jamaican events were the climax of the 1930s upsurge in the British West Indies. But there was to be one last flare-up of working-class resistance before the start of the Second World War. Four workers were killed and about a dozen injured during a strike at Plantation Leonora, British Guiana, in February 1939. This strike led to the recognition of the newly formed Manpower Citizens' Association.[17]

16
India

From the very beginning, the history of India under British rule is a history of resistance to that rule. Contrary to the myths, there never was a *pax Britannica* in India. Long before the national uprising of 1857–58 the peoples of India were harassing the invaders with a series of local uprisings. Some of these were spontaneous revolts by peasants against intolerable conditions. Others were risings by so-called 'primitive' peoples. Others again were connected with the Islamic revivalist organization known as the Wahhabis, which was not finally crushed until 1871. S. B. Chaudhuri, in a detailed study of civil disturbances in India between 1765 and 1857, discusses 23 uprisings in Bengal and Upper India, 12 in Madras and southern India, and 11 in Bombay and western India. Very seldom in that period, he writes, was the country free from disturbances: 'British government in India was like a house built over a mine of gunpowder.'[1]

As early as 1772–74 the Sannyasi uprising in the territory between Rangpur and Dacca threatened to sweep away British power. The rebels inflicted heavy defeats on the troops sent against them, and it was many years before they were finally suppressed.[2] Some 10,000 rebels in the 'protected' Travancore states revolted in 1804 against British influence there. The 1806 mutiny at Vellore, west of Madras, against new dress regulations that Indian soldiers saw as an affront to their religion, was in many ways a kind of rehearsal for 1857. The Jats rose at Biwani in 1809 and, with the Mewatis and Bhattis, again in 1824. The Gujars of Shahranpur rose in 1813 and again in 1824. British interference in the affairs of Kutch led, in the years 1815–18, to several risings aimed at driving the British out of Kathiawar. Kutch also saw rebellions by the Kolis in 1824, 1839 and 1844, and their resistance was not finally suppressed until 1848. About 8,000 Bhils, a people scattered through the Western Ghats and the neighbouring plains, rose in 1817–18 and again in 1819, 1831 and 1846. There were risings in Merwara (1820); Kittur (1824 and 1829); Savantvadi (1830, 1832 and 1836); Barasat (1831, a Wahhabi insurrection, brutally suppressed); Surat (1844, against an increase in salt duty); and Khandesh (1852). About 30,000 Santals, living on the plains skirting the Rajmahal Hills, rose in 1855–56 under the leadership of two brothers named Sidhu and Kanhu, who were said to have divine revelation.

The foregoing list is highly selective. It by no means exhausts the catalogue of Indian resistance before 1857. But enough examples have been given to show that British officers serving in India in that period were wise to sleep, as many did, with loaded pistols under their pillows.[3] And these 'frequent sporadic outbursts, often leading to serious armed resistance against the British authority ... culminated in the great upsurge of 1857 which shook the British empire in India to its very foundation'.[4]

Partly because it started as a revolt by Indian troops in the British army, partly because it suited the British to present it that way, the war of 1857–58 has generally been known in Britain as the 'Indian Mutiny'. Many Indian historians, reacting against this narrow and propagandist view, have presented it as India's first national war for independence. The truth lies somewhere between these two opposing views. What happened was much more than a soldiers' mutiny but rather less than a preconcerted war for independence. As soon as word spread that the sepoys had mutinied there was a series of peasant rebellions. These expressed both 'resentment at social displacement caused by [the peasants'] loss of land control', and grievances against excessive, differential taxation.[5] These local rebellions coalesced over a huge area into a general popular uprising, a full-scale Anglo–Indian war. The areas in revolt equalled in size France, Austria and Prussia together, and had a population of 45 million at a time when Britain was inhabited by 28 million people. Though Hindus and Moslems displayed remarkable unity – an aspect largely ignored by European historians[6] – the struggle threw up no nationalist leadership in the modern sense. Such leadership as did emerge was feudal in character, in the shape of local landowning monarchs unable for the most part to put the interests of the Indian people as a whole above their narrow personal ambitions. Thus the national rising of 1857–58 faced both ways: it looked back to India's past as well as forward to its future.

That the British, despite this lack of adequate leadership on the rebels' side, came 'within an ace of losing India'[7] cannot seriously be doubted. A British eyewitness wrote later that Britain's Indian empire 'all but disappeared'.[8] In many areas no visible symbol of the British *raj* was left. As for Britain's army in India, 'every regiment of regular cavalry, ten regiments of irregular cavalry out of eighteen, and sixty-three out of seventy-four regiments of infantry, then on the strength of the Bengal army, disappeared finally and completely from its roster!'[9]

The immediate cause of the army revolt was an insupportable religious grievance. Early in 1857 the British introduced a new breech-loading rifle whose cartridges were greased with animal fat. The sepoys were ordered to bite off the tip of each cartridge before inserting it into the open breech. The prospect of tasting pig fat horrified Moslems, while Hindus were no less horrified by the prospect of merely smelling grease from the sacred cow. On 9 May 1857 sepoys stationed at Meerut, having refused to load their rifles, were shackled by blacksmiths and put in prison cells. Next day, while their British officers were at church, three Indian regiments freed their imprisoned comrades, killed the officers who tried to stop them, burnt the officers' houses, and headed south with the cry 'To Delhi!' And Delhi, 30 miles away, undefended by a single British regiment, was taken within hours. Following this major blow to British prestige the revolt spread rapidly, soon embracing Lucknow and Cawnpore as well as the Gangetic plain – the heartland of north India – and, for a time, parts of the Punjab and Deccan. Everywhere government treasuries were plundered, magazines sacked, barracks, courthouses and other government buildings burnt down, prison gates flung open, and prisoners set free. Delhi was not recaptured until September; Lucknow and Cawnpore remained in rebel hands for six more months; and the uprising was not finally crushed until July 1858.

Among the humble and aristocratic participants in the national rising, one name stands out: Laxmi Bai, Queen (*Rani*) of Jhansi, India's Joan of Arc. The only rebel leader to die on the battlefield, this 23-year-old woman was cut down by a hussar while fighting, sword in hand, at the head of 1,500 men. Her two women friends, Mandar and Kashi, fought bravely by her side. Laxmi Bai's followers burnt the body so that the British should not boast that they had captured her dead. Colonel G. B. Malleson, in his *History of the Indian Mutiny* (1878–80), paid a chivalrous and deserved tribute to 'the resolute woman who, alike in council and on the field, was the soul of the conspirators', adding: 'Her countrymen will ever remember that she was driven by ill-treatment into rebellion, and that she lived and died for her country.'[10]

The rising was marred by the massacre at Cawnpore of 400 British men, women and children who had been promised safe conduct down the river to Allahabad. This atrocity was not committed by rebel troops, who had in fact disobeyed an order to fire on the unarmed garrison, but by a few personal followers of the disinherited prince Nana Sahib. The British took a ferocious and terrible revenge. Many thousands of unarmed Indians, including faithful domestic servants, were indiscriminately butchered, regardless of sex or age. At Delhi, many were shot as they clasped their hands for mercy, and many of those shot had all along been on the British side.[11] 'Hundreds of natives', admitted Sir Charles Dilke ten years afterwards, 'were hanged by Queen's officers who, unable to speak a word of any native language, could neither understand evidence nor defence.'[12] But all too often there was no trial at all. Sir John Kaye, in his standard *History of the Sepoy War in India* (1864–76), described how, between Umballah and Delhi, villagers were executed 'amidst every possible indignity that could be put upon them by our soldiers under the approving smiles of their officers'. In the Benares and Allahabad districts:

> our military officers were hunting down criminals of all kinds, and hanging them up with as little compunction as though they had been pariah dogs or jackals, or vermin of a baser kind ... Volunteer hanging parties went into the districts, and amateur executioners were not wanting to the occasion. One gentleman boasted of the number he had finished off quite 'in an artistic manner', with mango-trees for gibbets and elephants for drops, the victims of this wild justice being strung up as though for pastime, in 'the form of a figure of eight'.[13]

At Cawnpore, Brigadier-General James Neill forced high Brahmans to sweep up the blood of the murdered Europeans, then strung them up in a row without giving them the necessary time for the rites of purification. He made one lick part of the blood with his tongue, commenting: 'No doubt this is strange law, but it suits the occasion well, and I hope I shall not be interfered with until the room is thoroughly cleansed in this way.'[14]

Many of the captured rebel soldiers were strapped to cannon and blown to bits. A clergyman's widow described this as 'a most sickening sight', having seen a prisoner 'literally blown into atoms, the lookers on being covered with blood and fragments of flesh', while 'the head of one poor wretch fell upon a bystander and hurt him'.[15] A British lieutenant and the celebrated journalist W. H. Russell, in separate accounts, told how Englishmen and Sikhs, seizing one prisoner by the legs, tried to tear him in two. They then stabbed him repeatedly in the face with bayonets and finally burnt him alive. As he screamed and writhed in agony, his tormentors 'looked calmly on'. According to Russell, by a sudden effort he leapt away, 'and with the flesh hanging from his bones, ran for a few yards ere he was caught, brought back, put on the fire again, and held there by bayonets till his remains were consumed'.[16]

Why did the Indian national rising fail? Mainly because it was neither well organized nor well led. There was no overall plan of campaign. Those who emerged into leadership made two fatal mistakes: they failed to march swiftly east to take Calcutta; and they failed to prevent the movement of British troops from the Punjab, which was allowed to serve as a base from which the rising elsewhere was crushed. Moreover the British had better weapons (the newly invented Enfield rifle) and a superior method of communication (the telegraph).

Yet, though the rising was put down, resistance was kept alive in central India 'long after the British presence had been re-established and the principal leaders of revolt had submitted'.[17]

The cannonades suppressing the 'Mutiny' had hardly fallen silent when India's British rulers were faced with a new 'mutiny', within earshot of Calcutta. This was the so-called Blue Mutiny, already referred to (see p. 23 above). This movement against the indigo planters, whose entire industry 'ultimately rested on a foundation of coercion and intimidation',[18] began in the Nadia district, north of Calcutta. The cultivators in the village of Chaugacha took a vow never to plant indigo again, whereupon the planter sent a strong-arm squad to wreck the village. Over the next few years the movement against indigo cultivation spread throughout Nadia, Jessore, Patna, Maldah and Rajashahr. The villagers sent delegates to regional conferences, where the vow was reaffirmed. In Murshidabad thousands of peasants marched on the factories; the guards at one factory opened fire, killing two and wounding five. Villagers organized themselves into 'companies', each specializing in the weapon it found most suitable: spears, bows and arrows, slings, bricks, *lathis* (metal-tipped staves), brass plates thrown horizontally. The women threw earthen pots. To support this popular uprising against economic injustice, there was launched what has been called 'the precursor of all modern Indian political campaigns'. From this contest, writes Blair B. Kling, 'the Bengalis emerged with a heightened political awareness that prepared them, in the succeeding decades, to lead the rest of India in nationalist agitation'.[19]

But the nationalist movement that arose in Bengal was confined to a narrow social basis. It began as a revival of the Brahmo Samaj, a humanist reform movement originally created in 1828 by the poet, philosopher and journalist Raja Rammohan Roy. In 1866 Rajnarain Bose issued a prospectus for the establishment of a Society for the Promotion of National Feeling among the Educated Natives of Bengal, the object being to resist imitation of the West by reviving Hindu traditions in all fields. The great Bengali poet Rabindranath Tagore joined a secret society founded by Bose. Taking up Bose's ideas, Nabagopal Mitra, editor of the *National Paper* launched by Devendranath Tagore in 1865, started the Hindu Mela, an annual public gathering on the last day of the Bengali year, to promote national feeling and self-help. The patriotic songs and poems recited at these gatherings, including two by the 18-year-old Rabindranath Tagore, are still regarded as treasures of Bengali literature. Another revivalist movement was the Arya Samaj, founded in Bombay in 1875 by Dayanand Saraswati; this movement did no more than organize a network of schools and colleges, yet soon became a target of government repression. An India League was launched in Bengal in the same year. In 1876 an Indian Association was formed in Calcutta. This organized national conferences, mass meetings of peasants, 'rent unions', and night schools for adult education; it also sent agents to famine areas to collect information and, in conjunction with the Brahmo Samaj, opened relief centres in distressed villages.

Meanwhile discontent was growing in rural areas, especially after the agricultural depression of 1870 and the serious famines that followed it. In 1875 there were large-scale uprisings of peasants throughout the Poona and Ahmadnagar districts (the 'Deccan riots'). The people vented their fury against rapacious landlords, looting and burning their houses and shops and seizing mortgage bonds. Thirty-three villages were seriously affected; 951 persons were arrested and over 500 convicted. A leader known as Sivaji the Second, who claimed to be leading a national revolt, offered a reward of 500 rupees for the head of Sir Richard Temple, governor of Bombay. The rising was not put down until the entire military force at Poona, horse, foot and artillery, had taken the field against it.[20] A government commission of inquiry attributed the disturbances to the peasants' poverty and indebtedness. The terrible famine of 1876–77 led Wasudeo Balwant Phadke of Bombay to take a vow to stir up armed rebellion and destroy British power in India. Though he was arrested and transported to Aden for life, he had won wide popular support, and his methods of raising funds by robbery, secretly collecting arms, and training young men in their use, were to be copied by the revolutionary wing of the Indian nationalist movement a generation later.

By the 1880s India was in ferment. Fearing another national uprising on a still wider scale than that of 1857, Allan Octavian Hume, a British magistrate who had retired from the Indian Civil Service, took the initiative in organizing the Indian National Congress as a 'safety-valve for the escape of great and growing forces'.[21]

The Congress thus came into existence, in 1885, as an instrument to safeguard British rule in India. It was founded on the twin rocks of unswerving loyalty to the British Crown and the indissoluble partnership of the British Empire.[22] All the same, it is clear that without Hume's participation the authorities would have found some way to suppress the movement, a course they did in fact consider.[23] The English-educated liberal intellectuals who, under Hume's tutelage, led the Congress, hoped to persuade the British that their demands were reasonable rather than to rouse the Indians into political activity. Yet, to some extent, the Congress soon turned into a slightly less docile organization than its founders had expected. Some of its numerous pamphlets bitterly attacked the government. And the local political associations which became the regional arms of the Congress constituted a framework for the emergence of a mass movement. This development so alarmed the authorities that, as early as 1887, they set up an intelligence department, called the Special Branch, to keep an eye on all political, social and religious movements.

From the outset, the Congress was criticized – by, for instance, the nationalists Aurobindo Ghose (Sri Aurobindo) and Lajpat Rai, and the Bengal popular newspaper *Bangabasi*.[24] It was criticized for begging the British for more places in the Civil Service instead of arousing patriotism and concern for the lower classes. It was criticized for lack of contact with the masses. And it was criticized for in practice limiting its activities to the three days of its annual meeting. The first Indian leader to make a decisive break with the old nationalism was Bal Gangadhar Tilak, who conducted mass work among the victims of the 1896 Bombay famine. His emissaries explained to the people what their rights were under the Famine Relief Code and called on them to struggle for those rights. After serving a prison sentence for justifying political assassinations, in 1902 Tilak began openly hinting at civil disobedience, telling his audiences that they had the power to make India ungovernable if they chose.

Viceroy Curzon's partition of Bengal in 1905 was a great shock to Indians of all classes, and it fanned popular discontent into a conflagration. Partition was seen as a device to disrupt the Bengali people's political unity and, in particular, to drive a wedge between Hindus and Moslems. In the event it succeeded in uniting opposition to British rule. It gave tremendous impetus to the boycott of British goods and to the *svadeshi* movement for buying only goods made in India. So successful were these protests that in four years British imports slumped by more than a quarter. Though *svadeshi* cloth was coarser and dearer than that made in Lancashire, women and men alike wore it with pride as a badge of national devotion.

Under the impact of partition and the mass movement, the Congress split into two parties, known as moderates and extremists. The latter, known also as the New Party, had their strongholds in Calcutta, Poona and Lahore. They were led by Tilak, Rai, and Bipin Chandra Pal, who wanted to extend the boycott of British goods to British institutions, so as to make British rule impossible. In an atmosphere of mounting repression – widespread arrests, dispersal of public meetings, the stationing of military police in quiet areas, and frequent assaults on peaceful citizens – the 1907 session of the Congress broke up in disorder.

India's impatient youth now turned to bombs and pistols, in the belief that political assassinations of British officials would create an atmosphere favourable to armed insurrection. What they did bring about was still harsher repression coupled with a handful of minor concessions: the first Indian appointments to the Council of India (1907) and to the Viceroy's Executive Council (1909); the Morley-Minto reforms (changes to the composition and functioning of the legislative councils, 1909); and the partial reunification of Bengal (1911).

Immediately after the First World War the Indian national liberation movement began to gain a broad mass basis and to adopt the weapon of direct mass action. These developments were largely associated with the ascendancy of Gandhi and his strategy of non-violent non-cooperation. One of Gandhi's proposals that met with a wide response was that on a certain day the entire country should observe a *hartal*, that is, that everyone should stop work for a day and observe that day as one of fasting and prayer. Following this nationwide show of resistance to British rule came the massacre of unarmed demonstrators at Amritsar on 13 April 1919, when troops commanded by Brigadier Reginald Dyer fired for ten minutes into a dense crowd hemmed into a walled enclosure, killing 379 (according to official figures) and wounding 1,200. Martial law was proclaimed in the Punjab and there was a government reign of terror, with shootings, hangings, bombings from the air, and harsh prison sentences.

Despite his many shortcomings in ideology, strategy and tactics, Gandhi was the first Indian leader to recognize the role of the masses and of mass action in the freedom struggle. But the non-cooperation movement of the early 1920s depended too much on the efforts of one man, and it collapsed when Gandhi was imprisoned for sedition in 1922.

The early 1920s also saw the emergence of the All-India Trade Union Congress. Trade union activity in India before 1920 had been sporadic. There had been little strike activity, apart from a political general strike of Bombay textile workers in 1908 in protest at a sentence of six years' transportation imposed on Tilak for 'seditious' writings. A strike wave in the years 1918–20 affected Bombay, Calcutta, Madras, Cawnpore, Ahmedabad, and other industrial centres, and signalled the entry of the Indian working class into the liberation movement. Besides economic strikes, workers in Bombay and elsewhere staged political strikes against the Rowlatt Act, which gave the government power to imprison people without trial. Socialist ideas began to spread among India's radical youth, and Workers' and Peasants' Parties, precursors of the Communist Party of India, were formed in Bombay, Bengal and the Punjab.

After the breakdown of negotiations with the viceroy, Gandhi led another mass movement: the Civil Disobedience campaign of 1930. Foreign cloth was again boycotted. There were clashes between demonstrators and police, and an incident where a unit of Indian troops refused to fire on the crowds. Gandhi was again arrested, and it was estimated that 90,000 political prisoners were in jail in this period.

Released in 1931, Gandhi agreed to suspend the Civil Disobedience movement and participate in a Round Table Conference in London. When this failed, the Civil Disobedience movement was resumed, only to end finally in 1934. By now there was mounting criticism of Gandhi within the Congress. His leadership was seen as 'a peculiar blend of bold advances followed by sudden and capricious halts', of 'challenges succeeded by unwarranted compromises'.[25]

In 1936 the nationalist movement began to revive. The radical wing of the Indian National Congress was now stronger than ever, and the socialist Jawaharlal Nehru was elected Congress president. There was now a united peasant movement, the All-India Kisan Sabha, in whose activities the Communist Party of India played a prominent part. The trade union movement and the students' movement were both gaining ground. The Congress Socialist Party began to attract mass support. Congress ministries were formed in seven out of eleven provinces, and Congress membership soared from less than 500,000 at the beginning of 1936 to 5 million at the end of 1939.

When the Second World War began, both Gandhi and Nehru expressed sympathy for Britain, and Nehru said that India should offer Britain unconditional support. But Subhas Chundra Bose, a former Congress president and leader of the Forward Bloc, supported Congress resolutions opposing the use of India's resources in the interests of British imperialism, and his stand was backed by the Congress Working Committee. The Forward Bloc launched a new Civil Disobedience campaign. Many Congress supporters were arrested for shouting anti-war slogans. The arrest of Gandhi and all other Congress leaders in August 1942, Congress being declared an illegal body, led to violent mass demonstrations and strikes over nearly the whole of India.

In many areas there was a general uprising. About 250 railway stations were damaged or destroyed; many trains were derailed and many bridges blown up. Hundreds of post offices were attacked, and telephone and power lines were cut at 3,500 places. Seventy police stations were attacked; prisons were seized and prisoners set free. There were mass attacks on other government buildings. In many places the police retaliated by shooting down unarmed demonstrators. It was officially admitted that such firing took place on at least 538 occasions, and that 1,028 people were killed and 3,200 wounded; but Nehru estimated the number of deaths at about 10,000, and a Congress estimate put the figure at not less than 15,000.[26] Sixteen policemen were killed, and 332 injured, by the crowds. A total of 16,089 arrests were made.[27] One demonstration in Midnapore (Bengal) was led by a 73-year-old woman, Matangini Hazra, who was shot dead by troops. Revolutionary governments were set up, and independence declared, in Ballia, North Bhagalpur, and elsewhere. An anti-government radio station began broadcasting in Bombay; it transmitted news about the uprising until November 1942, when it was discovered and its operators arrested. The movement collapsed in the face of ruthless repression: over 60,000 people were arrested, many of whom were tortured in custody. Railway workers and villagers were machine-gunned from the air: 348 people were killed in air-raids in the Calcutta, Chittagong and Feni areas between 16 September 1942 and 10 February 1943.[28]

Though crushed by the full weight of British arms, this great upsurge of Indian resistance undoubtedly paved the way for Indian independence – as did the February 1946 mutiny by sailors of the Royal Indian Navy. This mutiny began when young ratings at the Bombay Signal School (HMS *Talwar*) staged a hunger strike in protest at what their central strike committee described as 'untold hardships regarding pay and food and the most outrageous racial discrimination' – and, in particular, against their commander's 'derogatory references to their national character'. The next day ratings from the *Talwar* sought and gained support from sailors elsewhere, who seized control of their ships, mounted the guns, and prepared to open fire on the military guards. 'Considerable alarm' was caused to the European community. In exchanges of fire between the sailors and British troops five Indians were killed and 36 wounded, and three British soldiers were wounded. There was unrest also in the Indian air force (described by Viceroy Wavell, in a letter to King George VI, as 'sullen and unstable for the most part') as well as in the army and police force, and there were demonstrations in Calcutta, Madras and Karachi, where eight demonstrators were shot dead by police and 18 injured. In Bombay a *hartal* (day of boycott) was organized in sympathy with the naval mutineers. The workers in almost all the Bombay mills came out, and there was widespread looting and burning: 30 shops, 9 banks, 10 post offices and 10 police stations (*chowkis*) were looted or destroyed. The workers put up road blocks and stoned those who tried to remove them. Police opened fire several times: 228 civilians and three policemen were killed; 1,046 civilians and 91 policemen were injured.[29]

The naval mutiny began on 18 February 1946. The following day the British government announced that it was sending a Cabinet Mission to India, to begin the negotiations that were to lead to independence the following year.

Conclusion

One result of the historical process described in this book is the black presence in the British Isles. Before the rise of capitalism this presence was tiny, fragmentary and discontinuous. Military and trading activities, between the third and fifteenth centuries AD, brought a trickle of individual Africans to end their days in these islands. The overseas expansion of British merchant capitalism gradually turned this trickle into a steady stream of young slave-servants from Africa, the West Indies, and India. By the second half of the eighteenth century Britain's black population numbered several thousands: at least 10,000, possibly somewhat more. Though this population dwindled in the course of the nineteenth century, there has been a continuous black presence in Britain for approximately 500 years.

Black migration to Britain after the end of the Second World War began in 1948, at first on a small scale. Settlers from the Caribbean were driven to Britain by the miserable conditions described in the Moyne Commission's report (see pp. 30–2 above). These conditions had worsened during the war. The cost of living had almost doubled in the British West Indies; there was large-scale unemployment, yet no relief of any kind for people without work. Recruitment campaigns encouraged West Indians to settle in Britain. Their labour was needed here. There was official encouragement, too, for settlers from the Indian sub-continent, impelled to seek a new life in Britain by the desperate poverty that was the chief legacy of Empire.

Despite this official encouragement, the entry into Britain of comparatively small numbers of black settlers – a few hundred in 1948–50, about 1,000 in 1951, about 2,000 in 1952 and again in 1953 – led to discussions in the Cabinet. The content of those discussions was not made public until the release of the relevant Cabinet papers in recent years - though Harold Macmillan had already revealed, in a volume of memoirs published in 1973, that early in 1955 Churchill proposed 'the cry of "Keep Britain White"' as 'a good slogan for the Election which we should soon have to fight without the benefit of his leadership'.[1] Churchill was in this period the pace-maker of state racism. As early as November 1952 he was asking whether the Post Office was employing 'large numbers of coloured workers. If so, there was some risk that difficult social problems would be created.'[2] Three weeks later the Cabinet asked the Home Secretary 'to arrange for officials of the Departments concerned to examine the possibilities of preventing any further increase in the number of coloured people seeking employment in this country'. At the same time the Chancellor of the Exchequer was asked to look into 'the possibility of restricting the number of coloured people obtaining admission to the Civil Service'.[3] And at roughly the same time Churchill was telling officials of the Ministry of Labour 'that he would not regard unfavourably proposals designed to restrict the entry of coloured workers into Great Britain'.[4] In the same period, discussing the settlement of black people in Britain, Churchill told Jamaica's governor, Sir Hugh Foot: 'We would have a magpie society: that would never do.'[5]

So there was set up a Cabinet Working Party on Coloured People Seeking Employment in the UK, one of three distinct working parties that gave consideration, in the years 1953–56, to what was seen at the highest level as an 'influx' of black people and a 'coloured invasion'. The Cabinet sought information from the police and the staffs of labour exchanges. The Metropolitan Police reported that 'on the whole coloured people are work-shy and content to live on national assistance and immoral earnings. They are poor workmen ... They are said to be of low mentality and will only work for short periods.' Police in industrial areas reported that 'coloured people generally are not suited to many forms of work'. Indians and Pakistanis were thought to be 'unscrupulous' and 'not usually a success in work requiring much skill or intellect'. In Newcastle, Glasgow and Nottingham the police condemned Asians as 'not engaging in any useful or productive work': they 'merely live on the community and produce nothing'. West Africans were described as 'lazy and arrogant': 'They associate with prostitutes and are confirmed gamblers.'[6] The police assured the Home Secretary that the practice of black men living on the immoral earnings of white women was 'much more widespread than the number of convictions would appear to indicate', and that 'coloured men play a large part in the illicit traffic in Indian hemp'.[7] According to Ministry of Labour informants, black workers were 'more volatile in temperament than white workers'. They found it hard to accept discipline and were more easily provoked to violence. In the Midlands the view was held by managers of labour exchanges that black workers were 'physically and temperamentally unsuited to the kind of work available in industrial areas'. As for black women,

> it is reported that they are slow mentally and find considerable difficulty in adapting themselves to working conditions in this country. The speed of work in modern factories is said to be quite beyond their capacity. On the other hand they have been found to give fairly reliable service as domestics in hospitals, institutions and private domestic employment.[8]

Some ministers seem to have been particularly exercised by the prospect of sexual relations between black people and white people. With evident relief the Committee of Ministers on Colonial Immigrants reported to the Cabinet in June 1956 that 'there seems to be little evidence at present of inter-breeding'. On the other hand, 'the indications that there is little inter-breeding at present cannot be projected to justify a forecast for the future. On present evidence a trend towards miscegenation can neither be forecast nor excluded. If such a trend were to occur it would be an important factor.' Another ministerial concern was the 'political consequences' of a concentration of black voters: 'It is not impossible that, in time, the vote of the coloured population might achieve a significance out of proportion to its size if it were concentrated in, say, half a dozen industrial towns involving twenty or twenty-five constituencies.'

With their minds clouded by this racist mishmash of immoral earnings, 'inter-breeding', cannabis, and black power, it is scarcely surprising that these ill-informed and, on the whole, rather stupid men found black settlement in Britain 'an ominous problem which cannot now be ignored'.[9] And this in spite of the evidence they also had in front of them, in the summer of 1956, that 'up till recently coloured immigrants have had little difficulty in finding work here'; that 'they have not made undue demands on National Assistance'; that 'they have created no particular problem in regard to the Health Service'; that 'they are generally law-abiding'; that, 'except in a few places, their presence has aroused little, if any, public expression of race feeling'.[10] Though they paid lip-service to these facts, the Cabinet still saw the entry of black people as 'an ominous problem'.

Again and again, at a time when black labour was being actively and eagerly recruited by such bodies as London Transport and the British Hotels and Restaurants Association, the Cabinet returned to its furtive discussion of how to stop the entry of black people with British passports ('undesirables') while not stopping that of white British subjects from the 'Old Commonwealth': Australia, Canada, New Zealand and Southern Rhodesia.[11] This was their great dilemma, as they freely admitted. 'It would obviously be impossible to discriminate openly against coloured people as such in administration or legislation in the field of employment', wrote the Home Secretary, David Maxwell Fyfe, in a memorandum dated 30 January 1954. There was, he continued, 'no effective means of stopping this influx' without giving immigration officers authority to refuse leave to land. And there could be no question of seeking such power to deal only with coloured people: it would have to be a power which could be exercised in relation to any British subject from overseas.'[12] Immigration control, said his successor Gwilym Lloyd-George ten months later, 'would have to be imposed on all British subjects alike', though it would be made to operate 'with the minimum of inconvenience' to those of them whose skins happened to be white.[13] Viscount Swinton, Secretary of State for Commonwealth Relations, was not convinced that legislation 'should be non-discriminatory in form'. 'We shall welcome', he wrote in a November 1954 memorandum, 'the comparatively few good young Canadians or New Zealanders who wish to work here, while restricting an excessive number of West Indians.' Other Commonwealth countries had this problem, he observed, and in some cases their legislation was non-discriminatory in form while their administration was discriminatory in practice – and 'we too shall have to discriminate in practice.'[14] In a later memorandum (June 1955) Swinton wrote of the 'large and continuing influx of coloured persons into this country'. There was no means of controlling this 'influx' without legislation. If such legislation extended to all British subjects without discrimination, some 'administrative easements' in favour of white immigrants would be needed.[15]

The chosen solution to the dilemma was a proposed system of work permits, which would be granted only to skilled workers. A prospective employer would have to seek permission for the entry of a named immigrant. This, it was thought, would both exclude almost all black immigrants and frustrate any accusations of discrimination on the grounds of colour. So assurances could readily be given that the policy was an impartial one. Immigration officials would have complete discretion to refuse entry to 'undesirables'. And the new regulations would be rigorously applied only at ports where immigrants from the Caribbean normally arrived.

Thus, in Edward Pilkington's words, 'by 1956 a full blue-print already existed for a racially discriminatory system of immigration controls'.[16] This blue-print was put into effect by the notorious Commonwealth Immigrants Act of 1962, the first in that long inglorious series of legislative measures that have made scarcely concealed racist discrimination part of the law of the land. The 1962 act restricted the admission of Commonwealth immigrants to those who had been issued with employment vouchers; made serious inroads into the civil rights of black British citizens whose passports had been issued outside the United Kingdom; and officially equated black skin with second-class citizenship. The unspoken assumption of the 1962 Act was the premise on which all the Cabinet discussions in the 1950s had been based: that the problem was not white racism, but the presence of black people in Britain. In 1962 racism was enshrined in British law for the first time. The Act's intention and effect were to restrict the entry of black people, though 'a certain pretence was maintained that the restriction was not in any particular way aimed at those who were not white, but this was done in a curiously formalistic way ... A transparent fiction was maintained, like an elaborate piece of Chinese etiquette, that this was neither its effect nor its purpose.'[17] And from that 1962 Act everything else has flowed. Concession after concession has been made to racism. So, 26 years later, we live in a racist society, which treats black people born in Britain as second-class citizens in the country of their birth. 'All strata of modern English society are infected, one way or another, with the racialist poison.'[18] We have a prime minister who fears 'that this country might be rather swamped by people with a different culture'.[19] We have had a junior minister in charge of ethnic monitoring in unemployment benefit offices who spoke of black people's countries of origin as 'Bongo Bongo Land'.[20] We have had a senior adviser on 'race relations' at the Home Office who, at a conference of the Police Federation, referred to black people as 'nig nogs'.[21] We have an operational chief of the Metropolitan Police's no. 6 area in west London who, discussing street signs for the 1986 Notting Hill carnival, said the signs should read: 'Coons go home.'[22] We had until recently a Metropolitan Police commissioner who told a respected American journalist that 'in the Jamaicans, you have people who are constitutionally disorderly ... It's simply in their make-up. They are constitutionally disposed to be anti-authority'.[23] We have a government that has rejected Lord Scarman's recommendation that racist behaviour should be made an offence under the police discipline code.[24]

From top to bottom, in belief and behaviour alike, the British police are racist. This was clearly shown by the Policy Studies Institute report on the Metropolitan Police, published in November 1983. Racist talk and racial prejudice, said this report, are 'expected, accepted and even fashionable'; 'one criterion that police officers use for stopping people, especially in areas of relatively *low* ethnic concentration, is that they are black'; 'police officers tend to make a crude equation between crime and black people, to assume that suspects are black and to justify stopping people in these terms'; 'to a considerable extent, police hostility towards people of West Indian origin is connected with the belief that they are rootless, alienated, poor, unable to cope and deviant in various ways'; police officers freely use such racist terms as 'coons', 'niggers', 'satchies', 'sooties', 'spades', 'monkeys', 'spooks', and 'Pakis'; 'we cannot produce examples of police officers objecting to racialist language'; 'apart from these casually abusive references, there is a vein of deliberately hostile and bitter comment on black people by police officers'; 'hostility to black people is linked, in the minds of these police officers, with racialist theories, right wing politics, fear of violence and disorder caused by black people, a psychological need for retribution and the view that violent retribution is legitimate.' And this damning report, the most extensive study of the Metropolitan Police ever carried out, concluded that 'the level of racial prejudice in the Force is cause for serious concern'.[25]

In April 1982 David and Lucille White, a black couple living in Stoke Newington, were awarded £51,392 in damages by a High Court judge after they had been brutally beaten by police. The judge said the 17 officers involved in the raid on their house, in September 1976, had been guilty of 'monstrous, wicked and shameful conduct'. The couple were subjected to a 'catalogue of violence and inhuman treatment by young officers'. The police had persisted in a five-year cover-up of their brutal, savage and sustained assaults. The judge said he could not accept police evidence of what happened. Several police officers who gave evidence were liars, and 'I regret to say I am forced to the conclusion that there has been an orchestrated attempt to mislead the Court in order to justify illegality and unjustified use of force.'[26]

In February 1986 Mrs Lorna Lucas, a black Sunday school teacher, won £26,000 damages from the Metropolitan Police for assault, false imprisonment and malicious prosecution. She had been assaulted by police who removed her forcibly from a builder's office where she had gone to make a complaint.[27]

In March 1986 Derek Pascal of Clapton was awarded £3,500 damages against Stoke Newington police. He had been beaten, punched, humiliated with racist abuse, burnt on the hand with a lighted cigarette, and forced to repeat: 'I am a black bastard.'[28]

There is a long and chilling list of black people who have died while in police custody or during police raids on their homes. Recent deaths in such circumstances include those of Eusif Ryan, Stephen Boyle, and Cynthia Jarrett (1985); Anthony Lemard and Ahmar Qureshi (1986); Clinton McCurbin, Ahmed Katongole, Nenneh Jalloh, and Anachu Anozie Osita (1987).

Encouraged by state racism and police racism, fascist gangs have in recent years stepped up their attacks on black people. A Home Office inquiry in 1981 showed that Asians were 50 times more likely to be attacked, and Afro-Caribbeans more than 36 times more likely to be attacked, than white people. Since 1977 there had been a fairly steady rise in the number of attacks reported. This Home Office report went on:

> The Asian community widely believes that it is the object of a campaign of unremitting racial harassment which it fears will grow worse in the future. In many places we were told that Asian families were too frightened to leave their homes at night or to visit the main shopping centre in town at weekends ... The frequency of such attacks, often of a particularly insidious nature, and the depth of feeling and concern which they generate in the ethnic minority communities, are a matter of fact and not of opinion. The minority communities ... were deeply troubled by the problem of racial attacks. There was a widespread sense of frustration at the apparent lack of positive response from the authorities.[29]

Two years later the Joint Committee against Racialism reported that 'the level of racialist violence has shown no noticeable reduction'.[30] A Greater London Council Police Committee report, issued at the end of 1983, confirmed that the level of racial harassment in London had increased over the previous two years. The police displayed a 'variety of non-responses', being reluctant to investigate, slow in getting on the scene, refusing to prosecute, giving misleading advice, and treating the victims of crimes as criminals themselves. In 1983, children had been shot at with airgun pellets; meat cleavers, Stanley knives, and fire-bombs had figured in the arsenal of racism; pensioners, students, shopkeepers and infants had been among the victims.[31]

The harassment continued in 1984. In Swindon an Asian family fled the country after a series of attacks on their home. In Newham a gang of white youths armed with pickaxes and sledge-hammers laid siege to an Asian family's home for an evening, bombarding it with bricks. An Asian minicab driver was murdered near Heathrow airport. In the Stepney area of east London gangs of up to 50 racists terrorized Asian families, and police called to help showed indifference or active hostility to the victims; private prosecutions brought because of police inaction ended in the victims being threatened with criminal charges for defending themselves. An Asian man in Woolwich had his eyes gouged out. An Asian man in East Ham had his jaw fractured and both arms broken at the wrist. Another was stabbed four times in the abdomen. At Stepney Green school, Tower Hamlets, a gang of 14 white youths attacked Mukith Mia, a 14-year-old Asian, as he walked back to school during the lunch-hour; they knocked him unconscious, then stabbed him twice, one cut being ten inches long down the centre of his back. In Bradford, Asian-owned shops were fire-bombed; in Manor Park a halal butcher's shop was reduced to rubble by an explosion.[32] Peter Burns, a black ticket collector at a station in Ilford, Essex, was taunted by several white youths, one of whom wrenched a spike from a nearby fence, plunged it into Burns's eye, and pierced his brain. Burns later died.[33] By 1984 some east London families were taking it in turns to stay up all night in case of racist attacks.

In December 1985 a mob of over 70 people went on a rampage through the Asian area of Keighley, damaging shops, homes, and cars, and hospitalizing at least four Asians.[34] In 1986 a 97-year-old Asian, Gulam Bham, on his way home from evening prayers at a Gloucester mosque, was hit from behind, then punched and kicked while on the ground. An Asian family in Wandsworth were forced out of their home after a prolonged campaign of harassment. Missiles had been thrown at the flat, dog shit pushed through the letter-box, their children threatened and racially abused; but the local housing department had refused to rehouse them. The Asian community in Grimsby were subjected to six days of terror.[35] A 13-year-old Bangladeshi schoolboy, Ahmed Iqbal Ullah, was stabbed to death at the gates of his school in Burnage, Manchester.[36]

In 1987 it was reported that one in four black residents of Newham had been the victim of a racist attack, and that four out of five of those who reported the attacks to the police were dissatisfied with their handling of the case.[37] Racist attacks in the Merseyside area reached record levels. Petrol bombings, 'where families had to flee and in which property was destroyed', were only part of the picture. Cars belonging to black people had been wrecked, the windows of their homes smashed, and people abused both in the street and in their homes. Shit and rats had been put through their letter-boxes. Single parents of black children had been the object of special attention. By now racist violence in south Leeds was so widespread that some Asian women, afraid to go into the street, were virtually prisoners in their own homes.[38] In Bradford and Grimsby, racist violence continued unabated, while in Scotland, according to the Scottish Asian Action Committee, racist abuse and attacks were taking place on an 'enormous scale'.[39]

In 1984 there were 7,000 recorded racist attacks in Britain. In 1985 the figure rose to 20,000. Since 1970 there have been more than 60 racist murders.[40]

Black people born in Britain are a permanent part of British society. They are here to stay. They will not put up with state racism, police racism, and racist harassment by fascist gangs. With ever-increasing determination they are defending themselves, their children, their homes, and their communities. In this task they have the support of all white people who have begun to understand the painful lessons, the painful truths, taught by black history.

Notes and References

Unless otherwise indicated, place of publication is London. The abbreviation PRO signifies Public Record Office.

Part I

Introduction

1. Edward Hallett Carr, *What is History?* (Macmillan, 1961), p. 37 (italics added).
2. Benjamin A. Quarles, 'Black History's Diversified Clientele', in *Africa and the Afro-American Experience,* ed. Lorraine A. Williams (Washington, D.C., Howard University Press, 1977), pp. 176, 182.
3. As quoted by Benjamin Quarles, 'Black History Unbound', in *Slavery, Colonialism, and Racism,* ed. Sidney W. Mintz (New York, W. W. Norton, 1974), p. 164.
4. Eugene D. Genovese, *In Red and Black: Marxian Explorations in Southern and Afro-American History* (Allen Lane, The Penguin Press, 1971), p. 247.
5. R. G. Collingwood, *The Idea of History* (Oxford, Clarendon Press, 1946), pp. 175, 230.
6. Cf. David Sutton, 'Radical liberalism, Fabianism and social history', in Centre for Contemporary Cultural Studies, *Making Histories: Studies in History-writing and Politics,* ed. Richard Johnson and others (Hutchinson, 1982), p. 16.
7. Right Rev. J. E. C. Welldon, 'Schoolmasters', in *Unwritten Laws and Ideals of Active Careers,* ed. E. H. Pitcairn (Smith, Elder, & Co., 1899), p. 284.
8. Lowell Ragatz, 'Must we rewrite the history of imperialism?', *Historical Studies – Australia and New Zealand,* VI/21 (November 1953), p. 92.
9. A. P. Newton, *A Hundred Years of the British Empire* (Duckworth, 1940), p. 12.
10. David Thomson, *England in the Nineteenth Century: 1815–1914* (Harmondsworth, Penguin Books, 1950), pp. 210–11 (italics added).

11. A. P. Thornton, *The Imperial Idea and its Enemies: A Study in British Power* (London, Macmillan & Co Ltd; New York, St Martin's Press; 1959), p. 209.
12. Cf. Gail Omvedt, 'Towards a theory of colonialism', *The Insurgent Sociologist*, III/3 (Spring 1973), p. 1. I am grateful to the British Library for obtaining a photocopy of this paper for me.
13. Rt Hon. Margaret Thatcher, M.P., foreword to Hugh Thomas, *History, Capitalism & Freedom* (Centre for Policy Studies, 1979). The Centre for Policy Studies was founded by Lord Cayzer, of British and Commonwealth Shipping, one of the biggest contributors to Conservative Party funds. Recent contributors to the Centre include Bowring Services, Beecham, the Rank Organisation, J. Lyons & Co., Plessey, the Hawker Siddeley Group, Glaxo, and De La Rue.
14. *The Times Higher Education Supplement*, no. 565 (2 September 1983), p. 24. See also, for a discussion of the issues raised, Roger Mettam and others, 'Forum', *History Today*, May 1984, pp. 5–16; I am grateful to Raphael Samuel for this reference.
15. Nigel Williamson, *The New Right: The Men behind Mrs Thatcher* (*Spokesman* Pamphlet no. 83, *Spokesman* and *Tribune*, 1984), pp. 7–8; *Economist*, CCXCIII/7362 (6 October 1984), p. 24.
16. *The Times*, 24 August 1984, p. 4.
17. For the military contribution of British black people, and black migrants in Britain, in two world wars, see: David Killingray, 'All the King's men? Blacks in the British Army in the First World War, 1914–1918', in *Under the Imperial Carpet: Essays in Black History 1780–1950*, ed. Rainer Lotz and Ian Pegg (Crawley, Rabbit Press, 1986), pp. 164–81; Marika Sherwood, *Many Struggles: West Indian Workers and Service Personnel in Britain (1939–45)* (Karia Press, 1984). For the contribution of Indian soldiers in two world wars, see Rozina Visram, *Ayahs, Lascars and Princes: Indians in Britain 1700–1947* (Pluto Press, 1986), pp. 113–43.

Chapter 1

1. E. G. R. Taylor, *Late Tudor and Early Stuart Geography 1583–1650* (Methuen & Co. Ltd, 1934), pp. 42–3.
2. Lewes Roberts, *The treasure of traffike: or a discourse of forraigne trade* (Nicholas Bourne, 1641), pp. 92–3.
3. John Strachey, *The End of Empire* (Victor Gollancz Ltd, 1959), p. 68.
4. E. J. Hobsbawm, 'The Crisis of The 17th Century – II', *Past & Present*, no. 6 (November 1954), pp. 56, 62.
5. Winston Churchill, as quoted by George Padmore, *The Gold Coast*

Revolution: The Struggle of an African People from Slavery to Freedom (Dennis Dobson Ltd, 1953), p. 16.

Chapter 2

1. Eric Williams, *British Historians and the West Indies* (André Deutsch, 1966), pp. 210–11; Eric Williams, *Inward Hunger: The Education of a Prime Minister* (André Deutsch, 1969), pp. 52–3. The publisher was Fredric Warburg.
2. Williams, *British Historians*, p. 233.
3. Christopher Fyfe, review of Roger Anstey, *The Atlantic Slave Trade and British Abolition, 1760–1810* (Macmillan, 1975), *Journal of African History*, XVII/1 (1976), p. 141.
4. Donald Woodward, 'The Port Books of England and Wales', *Maritime History*, III/2 (September 1973), p. 154.
5. Eric Williams, *Britain and the West Indies* (Longmans for the University of Essex, 1969), pp. 1, 2, 7 (italics added).
6. Richard B. Sheridan, 'The Plantation Revolution and the Industrial Revolution, 1625–1775', *Caribbean Studies*, IX/3 (October 1969), p. 5.
7. Cf. K. G. Davies, 'Essays in bibliography and criticism: xliv. Empire and capital', *Economic History Review*, 2nd ser. XIII (1960–61), p. 108.
8. Eveline C. Martin, 'The English slave trade and the African settlements', in *The Cambridge History of the British Empire*, I, *The Old Empire from the Beginnings to 1783*, ed. J. Holland Rose and others (Cambridge, University Press, 1929), p. 437.
9. [John Campbell], *Candid and impartial considerations On the Nature of the sugar trade* (R. Baldwin, 1763), p. 21.
10. Bryan Edwards, *The history, Civil and Commercial, of The British Colonies in the West Indies* (John Stockdale, 1793–1801), II, pp. 199–202.
11. A. P. Thornton, *West-India Policy under the Restoration* (Oxford, Clarendon Press, 1956), pp. 79–80.
12. [C. M. MacInnes], 'Bristol and overseas expansion', in *Bristol and its Adjoining Counties*, ed. C. M. MacInnes & W. F. Whittard (Bristol, for the British Association for the Advancement of Science, 1955), p. 227.
13. William Hunt, *Bristol* (Longmans, Green, & Co., 1887), p. 214.
14. [Patrick McGrath], 'Bristol since 1497', in *Bristol and its Adjoining Counties*, ed. MacInnes & Whittard, p. 214.
15. K. G. Davies, *The Royal African Company* (Longmans, Green, 1957), pp. 191, 166, 299. The figure of £500,000 for the value of the goods carried, cited in Peter Fryer, *Staying Power: The History of*

Black People in Britain (Pluto Press, 1984), p. 44, is an error.

16. Martin, 'The English slave trade and the African settlements', p. 445.
17. James A. Rawley, 'The port of London and the eighteenth century slave trade: historians, sources, and a reappraisal', *African Economic History*, IX (1980), pp. 85, 86, 93, 97–8. I am grateful to the British Library for obtaining a photocopy of this paper for me.
18. Herman Merivale, *Lectures on Colonization and Colonies* (Longman, Orme, Brown, Green, & Longmans, 1841–42), I, p. 295.
19. Michael J. Wise, 'Birmingham and its trade relations in the early eighteenth century', *University of Birmingham Historical Journal*, II (1949–50), p. 59.
20. G. Collins & M. N. Patten], 'Industry: the Technological Background', in *Swansea and its Region*, ed. W. G. V. Balchin (Swansea, University College of Swansea, 1971), p. 242.
21. William Enfield, *An essay towards the history of Liverpool* (Warrington, 1773), p. 89; Robert Norris, *A short account of the African slave trade* (Leverpool, printed at Ann Smith's Navigation Shop, 1788), p. 11.
22. Thornton, *West-India Policy*, pp. 80, 80 n.4.
23. Walter Rodney, *How Europe Underdeveloped Africa* (Washington, DC, Howard University Press, 1974), p. 96.
24. Walter Rodney, *West Africa and the Atlantic Slave Trade* (Lagos, Afrografika Publishers, [c. 1970]), p. 4.
25. Michael Craton, *Sinews of Empire: A Short History of British Slavery* (Temple Smith, 1974), p. 119.
26. Rodney, *How Europe Underdeveloped Africa*, p. 83. It should not be forgotten that the English slave trade began, not about 1630, but some 70 years earlier, with the pioneering ventures of Sir John Hawkyns. His three voyages in the 1560s attracted 'increasingly wealthy and powerful backers as the profit potential of the enterprises became apparent', and they netted profits estimated at between 40 and 60 per cent (Ronald Pollitt, 'John Hawkins's Troublesome Voyages: Merchants, Bureaucrats, and the Origin of the Slave Trade', *Journal of British Studies*, XII/2 (May 1973), pp. 27, 40). For the Guinea Company during the first half of the seventeenth century, see J. W. Blake, 'The farm of the Guinea trade', in *Essays in British and Irish History in Honour of James Eadie Todd*, ed. H. A. Cronne, T. W. Moody, and D. B. Quinn(Frederick Muller Ltd, 1949), pp. 86–106.
27. Rodney, *How Europe Underdeveloped Africa*, p. 80.
28. Walter Rodney, *A History of the Upper Guinea Coast 1545–1800*

(Oxford, Clarendon Press, 1970), p. 253.

29. Herbert J. Foster, 'Partners or Captives in Commerce? The Role of Africans in the Slave Trade', *Journal of Black Studies*, VI/4 (June 1976), p. 432.
30. Rodney, *A History of the Upper Guinea Coast*, p. 261.
31. In 1832 the Methodist preacher Henry Whiteley witnessed twenty formal floggings in seven weeks on a single estate in Jamaica. See Henry Whiteley, *Three months in Jamaica, in 1832: comprising a residence of seven weeks on a sugar plantation* (J. Hatchard & Son, 1833); W. L. Burn, *Emancipation and Apprenticeship in the British West Indies* (Jonathan Cape, 1937), p. 61.
32. Edwards, II, p. 498; Frank Wesley Pitman, *The Development of the British West Indies 1700–1763* (Yale Historical Publications, Studies IV, New Haven, Yale University Press, 1917), graph facing p. 168.
33. Pitman, p. vii.
34. Craton, p. 140.
35. Pitman, p. 30.
36. Douglas Hall, 'Absentee-proprietorship in the British West Indies to about 1850', *Jamaican Historical Review*, IV (1964), p. 16.
37. R. B. Sheridan, 'The rise of a colonial gentry: a case study of Antigua, 1730–1775', *Economic History Review*, 2nd ser. XIII (1960–61), p. 346.
38. Eugene D. Genovese, *The World the Slaveholders Made: two Essays in Interpretation* (Allen Lane the Penguin Press, 1969), p. 29.
39. John Gardner Kemeys, *Free and candid reflections Occasioned by the late additional duties on sugars and rum* (T. Becket etc., 1783), p. 58.
40. J. F. Reese, 'Mercantilism and the colonies', in *The Cambridge History of the British Empire*, I, p. 585.
41. E. J. Hobsbawm, 'The Crisis of The 17th Century – II', *Past & Present*, no. 6 (November 1954), p. 61.
42. [John Oldmixon], *The British Empire in America* (John Nicholson etc., 1708), II, p. 162.
43. For references, see Fryer, p. 467 n. 16.
44. For references, see Fryer, p. 467 n. 16.
45. For references, see Fryer, p. 468 n. 18.
46. Eveline C. Martin, *The British West African Settlements 1750-1821: a study in local administration* (Longmans, Green & Co. Ltd, 1927), p. 2.
47. [Sir Dalby Thomas], *An Historical Account of the Rise and Growth of the West-India collonies And of the Great Advantages they are*

to England, in respect to Trade (Jo Hindmarsh, 1690), p. 14.

48. *The importance of the Sugar Colonies to Great-Britain stated, and some Objections against the Sugar Colony Bill answer'd* (J. Roberts, 1731), p. 4.
49. *House of Commons Journals*, XXV (1745–50), p. 1003.
50. James Houston, *Some New and Accurate observations Geographical, Natural and Historical: Containing a true and impartial account of the Situation, Product, and Natural History of the Coast of Guinea, so far As relates to the Improvement of that Trade, for the Advantage of Great Britain in general, and the Royal African Company in particular* (J. Peele, 1725), pp. 43–4. See also *Memoirs of the Life and Travels of James Houstoun*, M.D. (J. Robinson etc., 1747), p. 147: 'This is a most beneficial Trade for the Nation in general, if rightly managed by exporting the Product and Manufactures of our Mother Country, and furnishing other *American* Colonies with *Negroes* cheaper than our Neighbours are able to do, and underselling them in foreign Markets.' The slave trade was 'one of the *best Branches* of our national Trade'.
51. [Campbell], pp. 21, 25, 218.
52. Norris, p. 11.
53. [John Hippisley], *Essays* (T. Lownds, 1764), pp. 17, 18.
54. Richard Sheridan, *The Development of the Plantations to 1750: An Era of West Indian Prosperity 1750–1775* (Chapters in Caribbean History, I, Caribbean Universities Press, 1970), p. 107.
55. *Lady Nugent's Journal of her residence in Jamaica from 1801 to 1805*, ed. Philip Wright (Kingston, Jamaica, Institute of Jamaica, 1966), pp. 62–3.
56. D. A. G. Waddell, *The West Indies & the Guianas* (Englewood Cliffs, N.J., Prentice-Hall, Inc., 1967), p. 53.
57. Cecil Northcott, *Slavery's Martyr: John Smith of Demerara and The Emancipation Movement 1817–24* (Epworth Press, 1976), p. 39.
58. Merivale, I, p. 82.
59. Eric Williams, 'The historical background of British Guiana's problems', *Journal of Negro History*, XXX (1945), pp. 371–2.
60. For child labour in Britain, see: J. L. Hammond and Barbara Hammond, *The Town Labourer 1760–1832: The New Civilisation* (Longmans, Green, & Co., 1917), pp. 143–93; E. P. Thompson, *The Making of the English Working Class* (Victor Gollancz Ltd, 1963), esp. pp. 331–49; David I. Gaines, 'Story of an English Cotton Mill Lad', *History of Childhood Quarterly: The Journal of Psychohistory*, II (1974–75), pp. 249-53.
61. Hammond and Hammond, *The Town Labourer*, p. 149.

62. J. L. Hammond and Barbara Hammond, *The Rise of Modern Industry* (Methuen & Co. Ltd., 1925), pp. 196–9.
63. *Memoirs of the Life of Sir Samuel Romilly, written by himself* (John Murray, 1840), II, pp. 372–3.
64. *Memoirs of the Life of Sir Samuel Romilly,* II, p. 393.

Chapter 3

1. Stanley Wolpert, *A New History of India,* second edition (New York & Oxford, Oxford University Press, 1982), pp. 147–8.
2. Major-General Sir John Malcolm, *The life of Robert, Lord Clive: collected from the family papers communicated by the Earl of Powis* (John Murray, 1836), II, p. 122.
3. Brooks Adams, *The Law of Civilization and Decay: An Essay on History* (Swan Sonnenschein & Co., 1895), p. 240.
4. L. C. A. Knowles, *The Economic Development of the British Overseas Empire* (George Routledge & Sons Ltd, 1924), p. 74.
5. Luke Scrafton, *Reflections on the government, &c. of Indostan* (A. Millar, 1763), p. 101.
6. Major Evans Bell, *Memoir of General John Briggs, of the Madras Army, with comments on some of his words and work* (Chatto & Windus, 1885), pp. 127–8. See also A. R. Desai, *Social Background of Indian Nationalism,* fifth edition (Sangam Books, 1984 reprint), pp. 38–58.
7. [Radha Kamal Mukherjee], 'Trade and industry', in *The Maratha Supremacy,* ed. R. C. Majumdar & V. G. Dighe (The History and Culture of the Indian People, VIII, Bombay, Bharatiya Vidya Bhavan, 1977), p. 776.
8. Romesh Dutt, *The Economic History of India under Early British Rule,* second edition (Kegan Paul, Trench, Trubner & Co. Ltd, 1906), pp. 23, 24.
9. William Bolts, *Considerations on India affairs, particularly respecting the present state of Bengal and its dependencies,* [vol. I] (J. Almon etc., 1772), pp. 191, 194.
10. Wolpert, 188. See also Narendra K. Sinha, *The Economic History of Bengal* (Calcutta, 1956–70), II, pp. 48–67.
11. *Ninth Report from the Select Committee, appointed to take into consideration the state of the administration of justice in the provinces of Bengal, Bahar, and Orissa* (1783), p. 45.
12. William Fullarton, *A View of the English Interests in India* (T. Cadell, 1787), pp. 40–1.
13. *Hansard's Parliamentary Debates,* 3rd ser. vol. 148 (1858), col. 1338.

14. Adams, p. 256.
15. William Digby, *'Prosperous' British India: a Revelation from Official Records* (T. Fisher Unwin, 1901), p. 33. For more recent discussions, see: Sinha, esp. I, pp. 210–19; and P. J. Marshall, *East Indian Fortunes: The British in Bengal in the Eighteenth Century* (Oxford, Clarendon Press, 1976).
16. Edward Baines, *History of the Cotton Manufacture in Great Britain* (H. Fisher etc., [1835]), p. 218.
17. *Report of the Indian Industrial Commission, 1916–18* (Cmd 51, 1919), p. 6.
18. Radha Kumud Mookerji, *Indian Shipping: a History of the Sea-borne Trade and Maritime Activity of the Indians from the Earliest Times*, revised edition (Bombay etc., Orient Longmans, 1957), pp. 178–80; [R. K. Mukherjee], 'Trade and industry', p. 779.
19. R. C. Majumdar and others, *An Advanced History of India*, second edition (Macmillan & Co., Ltd, 1950), p. 810; D. R. Gadgil, *The Industrial Evolution of India in Recent Times, 1860–1939*, fifth edition (Bombay etc., Oxford University Press, 1971), pp. 33–6.
20. See N. K. Sinha, *The Economic History of Bengal* (1956–70), III, pp. 1–25.
21. Frederick Clairmonte, *Economic Liberalism and Underdevelopment: Studies in the Disintegration of an Idea* (Asia Publishing House, 1960), p. 72.
22. Majumdar and others, p. 810.
23. C. C. Eldridge, *Victorian Imperialism* (Hodder & Stoughton, 1978), p. 63.
24. Horace Hayman Wilson, *The History of British India from 1805 to 1835* (Mill's *History of British India*, fourth edition, VII, James Madden & Co., 1845), pp. 538–9n.
25. Peter Harnetty, *Imperialism and Free Trade: Lancashire and India in the Mid-nineteenth Century* (Vancouver, University of British Columbia Press, 1972), pp. 34–5.
26. Wolpert, p. 248.
27. See B. N. Ganguli, *Dadabhai Naoroji and the Drain Theory* (Asia Publishing House, 1965). I am grateful to Rozina Visram for telling me about this book.
28. Daniel Houston Buchanan, *The Development of Capitalistic Enterprise in India* (New York, The Macmillan Company, 1934), pp. 36–8.
29. See *Report of the Indigo Commission* (House of Commons Accounts and Papers, 1861, XLIV).
30. Buchanan, pp. 52–3.

31. Dutt, p. vi.
32. *Report of the Indian Industrial Commission,* p. 257.
33. Vaughan Nash, *The Great Famine and its Causes* (Longmans, Green, & Co., 1900), pp. 245, 221.
34. Famine Inquiry Commission, *Report on Bengal* (Delhi, Manager of Publications, 1945), p. 107.
35. A. P. Thornton, *The Imperial Idea and its Enemies,* p. 228.
36. *Condition of India: Being the Report of the Delegation sent to India by The India League* (Essential News, [1934]), pp. 336, 344.
37. Isaiah Bowman, *The New World: Problems in Political Geography,* fourth edition (Yonkers-on-Hudson, NY, World Book Company, [1928]), pp. 99–100.
38. Jawaharlal Nehru, *The Discovery of India* (Meridian Books Ltd, 1946), pp. 247–8.
39. Reginald Reynolds, *The White Sahibs in India* (Martin Secker & Warburg Ltd, 1937), p. 93.
40. Jawaharlal Nehru, *An Autobiography: with Musings on Recent Events in India* (John Lane The Bodley Head, 1936), pp. 393, 399, 28, 435.

Chapter 4

1. Eric Williams, *From Columbus to Castro: the History of the Caribbean 1492–1969* (André Deutsch, 1970), p. 321.
2. William A. Green, *British Slave Emancipation: The Sugar Colonies and the Great Experiment 1830–1865* (Oxford, Clarendon Press, 1976), p. 112.
3. Williams, p. 329.
4. W. Emanuel Riviere, 'Labour shortage in the British West Indies after emancipation', *Journal of Caribbean History,* IV (May 1972), pp. 3–4.
5. Green, *British Slave Emancipation,* p. 171.
6. William A. Green, 'The West Indies and indentured labour migration – the Jamaican experience', in *Indentured Labour in the British Empire 1834–1920,* ed. Kay Saunders (London & Canberra, Croom Helm, 1984), p. 6.
7. Fred Sukdeo, 'The contribution of East Indians to economic development in Guyana' (paper presented to East Indians in the Caribbean, A Symposium on Contemporary Economics and Political Issues, University of the West Indies, 25–28 June 1975), p. 3.
8. Green, *British Slave Emancipation,* p. 279.
9. Hugh Tinker, *A New System of Slavery: the Export of Indian Labour Overseas 1830–1920* (Oxford University Press for Institute of

Race Relations, 1974), pp. 199–200.

10. K. O. Laurence, *Immigration into the West Indies in the 19th Century* (Chapters in Caribbean History, 3, St Lawrence, Barbados, Caribbean Universities Press, 1971), p. 51.
11. Tinker, p. xiii.
12. Laurence, p. 53.
13. Tinker, pp. xiv–xv.
14. For indentured labour in the British West Indies, see also: C. Kondapi, *Indians Overseas 1838–1949* (New Delhi, Indian Council of World Affairs; Bombay etc., Oxford University Press; 1951); I. M. Cumpston, *Indians Overseas in British Territories 1834–1854* (Oxford University Press, 1953); Dwarka Nath, *A History of Indians in British Guiana* (Thomas Nelson & Sons Ltd, 1950); R. C. Majumdar, 'Indian serfs and slaves in the British Empire', in *British Paramountcy and Indian Renaissance*, pt 2, ed. R. C. Majumdar (The History and Culture of the Indian People, X, Bombay, Bharatiya Vidya Bhavan, 1965), pp. 617–25; Judith Ann Weller, *The East Indian Indenture in Trinidad* (Caribbean Monograph Ser. no. 4, Rio Piedras, Puerto Rico, Institute of Caribbean Studies, University of Puerto Rico, 1968); Marianne D. Ramesar, 'Indentured labour in Trinidad, 1880–1917', in *Indentured Labour in the British Empire*, ed. Saunders, pp. 57–77.
15. W. L. Burn, *Emancipation and Apprenticeship in the British West Indies* (1937), p. 279.
16. Burn, p. 280.
17. Burn, p. 282.
18. Vere T. Daly, *A Short History of the Guyanese People* (Macmillan Education, 1975), p. 202.
19. Daly, p. 206.
20. *Hansard's Parliamentary Debates*, 3rd ser. vol. 151 (1858), col. 2100.
21. *Report of the Royal Commission appointed ... to inquire into the public revenues, expenditure, debts, and liabilities of the islands of Jamaica, Grenada*, etc., pt IV, Supplementary Remarks (C. 3840-III, 1884), pp. 17, 16.
22. *Report of the West India Royal Commission* (C. 8655, 1897), p. 64.
23. Williams, pp. 450, 451, 454.
24. *Report of the West India Royal Commission, 1938–1939* (Cmd 6607, 1944–45), pp. 32, 34, 92, 139, 174.

Chapter 5

1. W. Rodney, *How Europe Underdeveloped Africa* (1974), pp. 103–4.
2. H[illaire]. B[elloc]. and B. T. B. [i.e. Lord Ian B. G. T. Blackwood], *The Modern Traveller* (Edward Arnold, 1898), p. 41.
3. John M. MacKenzie, *The Partition of Africa 1880–1900 and European Imperialism in the Nineteenth Century* (Lancaster Pamphlets, London & New York, Methuen, 1983), p. 1.
4. J. Scott Keltie, *The Partition of Africa* (Edward Stanford, 1893), p. 1.
5. P. A. Bower and others, *Mining, Commerce and Finance in Nigeria,* ed. Margery Perham (Faber & Faber Limited, 1948), Table IV, pp. 28–9; Rodney, p. 150.
6. Bower and others, Table II, pp. 18–19.
7. Rodney, p. 151.
8. 'African copper', *Empire,* I/2 (July 1938), p. 22; Leonard Barnes, *Empire or Democracy? A Study of the Colonial Question* (Victor Gollancz Ltd, 1939), p. 153.
9. Rodney, p. 151.
10. Rodney, p. 154.
11. Rodney, p. 166.
12. Rodney, p. 169.
13. Mary H. Kingsley, *Travels in West Africa: Congo Français, Corisco and Cameroons* (Macmillan & Co. Limited, 1897), p. 691.
14. *Colonialism in Africa 1870–1960,* IV, The Economics of Colonialism, ed. Peter Duignan and L. H. Gann (Cambridge University Press, 1975), p. 689.
15. Kwame Nkrumah, *Africa Must Unite* (Heinemann, 1963), pp. 26–31.
16. *Fifth Report from the Select Committee on Estimates: Session 1947–48: Colonial Development* (HMSO, 1948), p. xix.

Chapter 6

1. M. M. Bennett, *The Australian Aboriginal as a Human Being* (Alston Rivers Ltd, 1930), p. 39.
2. For black Tasmanians, see: W. E. L. H. Crowther, '1803–1876: the passing of the Tasmanian race', *Medical Journal of Australia,* 21st year, i/5 (3 February 1934), pp. 147–60; Clive Turnbull, *Black War: The Extermination of the Tasmanian Aborigines* (Melbourne & London, F. W. Cheshire, 1948); *Friendly mission: The Tasmanian Journals and Papers of George Augustus Robinson 1829–1834,* ed. N. J. B. Plomley ([Hobart], Tasmanian Historical Research Association, 1966); C. D. Rowley, *The Destruction of Aboriginal Society* (Aboriginal policy and practice, I; Aborigines in Australian Society, 4; Canberra, Australian National

University Press, 1970), pp. 43–53; Clive Turnbull, 'Tasmania: the ultimate solution', in *Racism: The Australian Experience: A Study of Race Prejudice in Australia*, ed. F. S. Stevens, II, Black versus white (Sydney, Australia & New Zealand Book Company, 1972), pp. 228–34; David Davies, *The Last of the Tasmanians* (Frederick Muller, 1973); N. J. B. Plomley, *The Tasmanian Aborigines: a Short Account of Them and Some Aspects of Their Life* (Launceston, Tasmania, the Author in association with the Adult Education Division, 1977); Lloyd Robson, *A History of Tasmania*, I, Van Diemen's Land from the Earliest Times to 1855 (Melbourne etc., Oxford University Press, 1983), pp. 13–31, 45–51, 210–53, 531–4. For further references, see N. J. B. Plomley, *An Annotated Bibliography of the Tasmanian Aborigines* (Royal Anthropological Institute Occasional Paper no. 28, Royal Anthropological Institute of Great Britain & Ireland, 1969).

3. Rowley, *The Destruction of Aboriginal Society*, pp. 13, 15.
4. Thomas Dunbabin, *The Making of Australasia: a Brief History of the Origin and Development of the British Dominions in the South Pacific* (A. & C. Black, Ltd., 1922), p. 110; A. Grenfell Price, *White Settlers and Native Peoples: An Historical Study of Racial Contacts between Whites and Aboriginal Peoples in the United States, Canada, Australia and New Zealand* (Melbourne, Georgia House; Cambridge, University Press; 1950), p. 107.
5. Paul Hasluck, *Black Australians: a Survey of Native Policy in Western Australia, 1829–1897* (Melbourne & London, Melbourne University Press in association with Oxford University Press, 1942), p. 168.
6. For black Australians, see also: Price, pp. 99–149; C. D. Rowley, *Outcasts in White Australia* (Aboriginal policy and practice, II; Aborigines in Australian society, 6; Canberra, Australian National University Press, 1971); C. D. Rowley, *The Remote Aborigines* (Aboriginal policy and practice, III; Aborigines in Australian society, 7; Canberra, Australian National University Press, 1971); *Racism: The Australian Experience*, ed. F. S. Stevens, II (1972); Peter Biskup, *Not Slaves not Citizens: The Aboriginal Problem in Western Australia 1898–1954* (St Lucia, Queensland, University of Queensland Press; New York, Crane, Russak & Company, Inc.; 1973); Fergus Robinson and Barry York, *The Black Resistance: An Introduction to the History of the Aborigines' Struggle against British Colonialism* (Camberwell, Victoria, Widescope, 1977); Janine Roberts, *From Massacres to Mining: The Colonization of Aboriginal Australia* (CIMRA & War on Want, 1978); Henry

Reynolds, *The Other Side of the Frontier: Aboriginal Resistance to the European Invasion of Australia* (Ringwood, Victoria, Penguin Books Australia Ltd, 1982); Raymond Evans, '"Kings" in brass crescents: defining Aboriginal labour patterns in colonial Queensland', in *Indentured Labour in the British Empire*, ed. K. Saunders (1984), pp. 183–212. The current situation is described in Jon C. Altman and John Nieuwenhuysen, *The Economic Status of Australian Aborigines* (Cambridge University Press, 1979); I am grateful to H. O. Nazareth for telling me about this book and those by Robinson and York and by Roberts above.

7. M. P. K. Sorrenson, 'Maori and Pakeha', in *The Oxford History of New Zealand*, ed. W. H. Oliver and B. R. Williams (Oxford, Clarendon Press; Wellington, Oxford University Press; 1981), p. 169.
8. John Miller, *Early Victorian New Zealand: A Study of Racial Tension and Social Attitudes 1839–1852* (Oxford University Press, 1958), p. vii.
9. Sorrenson, 'Maori and Pakeha', p. 192.
10. William Fox, *The Six Colonies of New Zealand* (John W. Parker & Son, 1851), p. 52.
11. As quoted by Miller, p. 104.
12. Alfred K. Newman, 'A Study of the Causes leading to the Extinction of the Maori', *Transactions and Proceedings of the New Zealand Institute*, XIV (1881), p. 477.
13. Archdeacon Walsh, 'The Passing of the Maori: An Inquiry into the Principal Causes of the Decay of the Race', *Transactions and Proceedings of the New Zealand Institute*, XL (1907), p. 154.
14. For the Maoris, see also: *The Maori People Today: a General Survey*, ed. I. L. G. Sutherland (New Zealand Institute of International Affairs & New Zealand Council for Educational Research, 1940); A. G. Price, *White Settlers and Native Peoples* (1950), pp. 150–88; Keith Sinclair, *The Origins of the Maori Wars* (Wellington, New Zealand University Press, 1957); Alan D. Ward, 'Brown Man's Burden: The Maoris Today', *Dissent* (Melbourne), no. 23 (Spring 1968), pp. 27–34; Ian Wards, *The Shadow of the Land: a Study of British Policy and Racial Conflict in New Zealand 1832–1852* (Wellington, Historical Publications Branch, Department of Internal Affairs, 1968); Alan Ward, *A Show of Justice: Racial 'Amalgamation' in Nineteenth Century New Zealand* ([Auckland], Auckland University Press & Oxford University Press, 1974); M. P. K. Sorrenson, 'How to Civilize Savages: some "answers" from nineteenth-century New Zealand', *New Zealand Journal of History*, IX (1975), pp. 97–110; Peter

Adams, *Fatal Necessity: British Intervention in New Zealand 1830–1847* ([Auckland], Auckland University Press & Oxford University Press, 1977); D. Ian Pool, *The Maori Population of New Zealand 1769–1971* ([Auckland], Auckland University Press & Oxford University Press, 1977).

15. Leonard Thompson, 'Co-operation and conflict: the Zulu kingdom and Natal', in *The Oxford History of South Africa,* ed. Monica Wilson and L. Thompson, I (Oxford, Clarendon Press, 1973 reprint), pp. 376, 387.
16. John Addison, *Apartheid* (Batsford Academic & Educational Ltd, 1981), p. 14.
17. C. W. De Kiewiet, *A History of South Africa: Social & Economic* (Oxford, Clarendon Press, 1941), p. 74; T. R. H. Davenport, *South Africa: A Modern History,* 2nd edition (Macmillan, 1978), p. 332. For Sir Theophilus Shepstone, see also: Edgar H. Brookes, *The History of Native Policy in South Africa from 1830 to the Present Day* (Cape Town, Nasionale Pers, 1924), pp. 41–86; J. R. Sullivan, *The Native Policy of Sir Theophilus Shepstone* (Johannesburg, Walker & Snashall, Ltd, 1928); C. J. Uys, *In the Era of Shepstone: being a Study of British Expansion in South Africa (1842–1877)* (Lovedale, Lovedale Press, 1933); Alan F. Hattersley, *Portrait of a Colony: The Story of Natal* (Cambridge, University Press, 1940), pp. 203ff.; R. E. Gordon, *Shepstone: the Role of the Family in the History of South Africa* (Cape Town, A. A. Balkema, 1968).
18. Earl Grey to Governor Sir H. G. Smith, Bart., 30 November 1849, in *Correspondence relating to the Settlement of Natal* (Parliamentary Papers, 1850, XXXVIII), p. 198.
19. Earl Grey, *The Colonial Policy of Lord John Russell's Administration* (Richard Bentley, 1853), II, p. 259.
20. W. M. Macmillan, *Bantu, Boer and Briton: The Making of the South African Native Problem,* revised and enlarged edition (Oxford, Clarendon Press, 1963), pp. 340, 341.
21. Hilda Kuper, *An African Aristocracy: Rank among the Swazi of Bechuanaland* (Oxford University Press for International Affairs Institute, 1947), p. 24; L. Thompson, 'The subjection of the African chiefdoms', in *The Oxford History of South Africa,* ed. Wilson and Thompson, II (Oxford, Clarendon Press, 1978 reprint), p. 275.
22. Sarah Gertrude Millin, *Rhodes* (Chatto & Windus, 1933), p. 229.
23. George McCall Theal, *History of South Africa from 1873 to 1884* (George Allen & Unwin Ltd, 1919), I, p. 175.
24. Thompson, p. 281.
25. Cf. Bernard Makhosezwe Magubane, *The Political Economy of*

Race and Class in South Africa (New York & London, Monthly Review Press, 1979), p. 38.

26. *The Milner Papers,* II, South Africa 1899–1905, ed. Cecil Headlam (Cassell & Co Ltd, 1933), pp. 35, 307.
27. *Selections from the Smuts Papers,* II (June 1902–May 1910), ed. W. K. Hancock and Jean van der Poel (Cambridge, University Press, 1966), pp. 377–8.
28. Ronald Hyam, *Britain's Imperial Century 1815–1914: A Study of Empire and Expansion* (B. T. Batsford, 1976), p. 298.
29. Hyam, p. 298.
30. Hyam, pp. 298–9.
31. Francis Wilson, 'Farming 1866–1966', in *The Oxford History of South Africa,* ed. M. Wilson and Thompson, II, pp. 129–30. See also: Sol. T. Plaatje, *Native Life in South Africa, before and since the European War and the Boer Rebellion* (P. S. King & Son, Ltd, 1916), p. 53; C. M. Tatz, *Shadow and Substance in South Africa: A Study in Land and Franchise Policies Affecting Africans, 1910–1960* (Pietermaritzburg, University of Natal Press, 1962), esp. pp. 17–22.
32. Tatz, p. 22.
33. F. Wilson, p. 131.
34. Kay Saunders, 'The workers' paradox: indentured labour in the Queensland sugar industry to 1920', in *Indentured Labour in the British Empire,* ed. Saunders, p. 230. For indentured labour in Australia, see also C. Kondapi, *Indians Overseas 1838–1949* (1951), pp. 192–3, and H. Tinker, *A New System of Slavery* (1974), pp. 69, 264–5, 271–2.
35. Maureen Tayal, 'Indian Indentured Labour in Natal, 1890–1911', *Indian Economic and Social History Review,* XIV (1977), p. 539. For indentured labour in South Africa, see also: Kondapi, *passim;* L. M. Thompson, 'Indian immigration into Natal (1860–1872)', *Archives Year Book for South African History,* 15th year (1952), vol. ii, pp. vii–76; Mabel Palmer, *The History of the Indians in Natal* (Natal Regional Survey, X, Cape Town etc., Oxford University Press, 1957); *The Oxford History of South Africa,* ed. M. Wilson and L. Thompson, I (Oxford, Clarendon Press, 1973 reprint), pp. 387–90, II, pp. 236–7; Tinker, *passim.*
36. Tinker, p. 57; Ravindra K. Jain, 'South Indian labour in Malaya, 1840–1920: asylum stability and involution', in *Indentured Labour in the British Empire,* ed. Saunders, pp. 158–82.
37. Kondapi, pp. 25–9; Tinker, pp. 57–8, 59, 263–4; Brij V. Lal, 'Labouring men and nothing more: some problems of Indian indenture in Fiji', in *Indentured Labour in the British Empire,* ed.

Saunders, pp. 126–57.

38. Kondapi, pp. 8–16; Tinker, pp. 54–6; Burton Benedict, 'Slavery and Indenture in Mauritius and Seychelles', in *Asian and African Systems of Slavery*, ed. James L. Watson (Oxford, Basil Blackwell, 1980), pp. 135–68; M. D. North-Coombes, 'From slavery to indenture: forced labour in the political economy of Mauritius 1834–1867', in *Indentured Labour in the British Empire*, ed. Saunders, pp. 78–125.

Chapter 7

1. Richard Pares, 'The economic factors in the history of the Empire', *Economic History Review*, VII (1936–37), p. 120.
2. This paragraph owes much to Jack Woddis, *An Introduction to Neo-colonialism* (Lawrence & Wishart, 1967).
3. Captain F. D. Lugard, *The Rise of our East African Empire: Early Efforts in Nyasaland and Uganda* (Edinburgh & London, William Blackwood & Sons, 1893), I, p. 381.
4. *Journal of the Royal Colonial Institute*, XXIV (1892–93), p. 315.
5. *Parliamentary Debates*, 4th ser. vol. 36 (1895), col. 641–2.

Chapter 8

1. Margery Perham, Introduction to Robert Heussler, *Yesterday's Rulers: The Making of the British Colonial Service* (Syracuse University Press & Oxford University Press, 1963), p. xix.
2. A. P. Thornton, *For the File on Empire: Essays and Reviews* (Macmillan, 1968), pp. 352–4.
3. Heussler, pp. 96–8. See also Rupert Wilkinson, *The Prefects: British Leadership and the Public School Tradition: A Comparative Study in the Making of Rulers* (Oxford University Press, 1964), pp. 100–9.
4. Heussler, p. 101.
5. E. K. Lumley, *Forgotten Mandate: a British District Officer in Tanganyika* (C. Hurst & Company, 1976), p. 64.
6. Lumley, p. 55.
7. Honble Frederick John Shore, *Notes on Indian Affairs* (John W. Parker, 1837), I, pp. 10–11.
8. Charles Wentworth Dilke, *Greater Britain: a Record of Travel in English-speaking Countries during 1866 and 1867* (Macmillan & Co, 1868), II, pp. 224–5.
9. James Routledge, *English Rule and Native Opinion in India: from Notes taken 1870–74* (Trübner & Co., 1878), p. 278.
10. H. J. S. Cotton, *New India or India in Transition* (Kegan Paul,

Trench, & Co., 1885), pp. 41, 42, 37.

11. *The letters of Queen Victoria,* third ser., ed. George Earle Buckle (John Murray, 1930–32), III, p. 251; David Dilks, *Curzon in India* (Rupert Hart-Davis, 1969–70), I, p. 240.
12. Robert V. Kubicek, *The Administration of Imperialism: Joseph Chamberlain at the Colonial Office* (Duke University Commonwealth Studies Center ser. no. 37, Durham, NC, Duke University Press, 1969), p. 35.
13. As quoted by Kubicek, pp. 34–5.
14. *Correspondence relating to the Flogging of Natives by Certain Europeans in Nairobi* (Cd 3562, 1907); George Bennett, 'Settlers and Politics in Kenya', in *History of East Africa,* ed. Vincent Harlow and E. M. Chilver (Oxford, Clarendon Press, 1965), p. 276; G. N. Mungeam, *British Rule in Kenya 1895–1912: the Establishment of Administration in the East African Protectorate* (Oxford, Clarendon Press, 1966), p. 184.
15. Ian Duffield, 'John Eldred Taylor and West African opposition to indirect rule in Nigeria', *African Affairs,* LXX (1971), p. 255.
16. H. Alan C. Cairns, *Prelude to Imperialism: British Reactions to Central African Society 1840–1890* (Routledge & Kegan Paul, 1965), p. 45.

Chapter 9

1. W. T. Stead, *The History of the Mystery; or, The Story of the Jameson Raid* (Masterpiece Library, 58, *Review of Reviews* office, 1897), pp. 3–4. I am grateful to Alan Unwin for obtaining for me a photocopy of this reference. This is the source of the familiar quotation attributed to Rhodes in Lenin's *Imperialism, the Highest Stage of Capitalism;* cf. V. I. Lenin, *Collected Works,* XXII, pp. 256–7.
2. William G. Hynes, *The Economics of Empire: Britain, Africa and the New Imperialism 1870–95* (Longman, 1979), p. 139.
3. John M. MacKenzie, *Propaganda and Empire: The Manipulation of British Public Opinion, 1880–1960* (Manchester University Press, 1984), p. 18. I am grateful to Paul Gilroy for telling me about this book.
4. W. A. Green, *British Slave Emancipation* (1976), p. 94; cf. Very Revd Ignatius Scoles, *Sketches of African and Indian Life in British Guiana* [second edition] (Demerara, 'Argosy' Press, 1885), p. 66. A well-dressed woman coming away from the 1924–5 Empire exhibition at Wembley was heard to tell another how impressed she had been with the 'Chinese' pavilion, meaning the Hong Kong

one; to which her friend replied: 'I think you mean Japanese, my dear; China doesn't yet belong to us.' The Empire Marketing Board, set up in 1926 to push Empire wares, was constantly finding shopkeepers and customers who thought Californian tinned fruit was one (Rt Hon. L. S. Amery, *My Political Life*, II, War and Peace 1914-1929 [Hutchinson, 1953], p. 340).

5. *The Times*, 22 June 1949, p. 4.
6. Lionel Curtis, *World War: Its Cause and Cure* (Oxford University Press, 1945), p. 191; W. E. F. Ward, 'The Colonial Phase in British West Africa, (i) The Period of Direct Rule', in *A Thousand Years of West African History: A Handbook for Teachers and Students*, ed. J. F. Ade & Ian Espie (Ibadan University Press & Nelson, 1965), p. 405.
7. See Bernard Porter, *Critics of Empire: British Radical Attitudes to Colonialism in Africa 1895–1914* (Macmillan, 1968), pp. 96, 105.
8. Partha Sarathi Gupta, *Imperialism and the British Labour Movement, 1914–1964* (Cambridge Commonwealth ser., Macmillan, 1975), p. 8.
9. Henry Mayers Hyndman, *Further Reminiscences* (Macmillan & Co., Limited, 1912), p. 151.
10. J. M. MacKenzie, *The Partition of Africa* (1983), p. 36.
11. Major-General Sir Frederick Maurice, *Haldane 1915–1928: The Life of Viscount Haldane of Clain K.T., O.M.* (Faber & Faber Limited, 1939), 152; cf. Gregory Blaxland, *J. H. Thomas: a Life for Unity* (Frederick Muller Limited, 1964), 170. For Thomas's views on colonialism and the 'natives', see J. H. Thomas, *My Story* (Hutchinson & Co., 1937), p. 81.
12. Gupta, p. 11.
13. *Fabianism and the Empire: a manifesto by the Fabian Society*, ed. Bernard Shaw (Grant Richards, 1900), pp. 21ff., 15; A. P. Thornton, *The imperial idea and its enemies* (1959), p. 76.
14. Gupta, p. 11; *The Diary of Beatrice Webb*, II, 1892–1905: 'All the Good Things of Life', ed. Norman and Jeanne MacKenzie (Virago, 1983), p. 188.
15. A. M. McBriar, *Fabian Socialism and English Politics 1884–1918* (Cambridge, University Press, 1962), pp. 126, 130, 134.
16. L. Haden Guest, *The Labour Party & the Empire* (Labour Publishing Company Ltd, 1926),p. 7. For Labour Party and Trades Union Congress attitudes towards, and policies on, the British Empire, see also Bernard Semmel, *Imperialism and Social Reform: English Social-Imperial Thought 1895–1914* (Studies in society, no. 5, George Allen & Unwin Ltd, 1960).

17. Robert Gray, *The Aristocracy of Labour in Nineteenth-Century Britain* c. *1850–1900* (Studies in Economic and Social History, Macmillan, 1981), pp. 54–5.
18. Lord Rosebery, *Questions of Empire* (Arthur L. Humphreys, 1900), p. 37.
19. Hon. George Curzon, *Problems of the Far East: Japan – Korea – China* (Longmans, Green, & Co., 1894), dedication.
20. *Transactions of the Aborigines Protection Society,* 1896–1900, p. 38.

Part II

Chapter 10

1. M. F. Ashley Montagu, *Man's most Dangerous Myth: The Fallacy of Race* (New York, Columbia University Press, 1942), p. 36.
2. L. S. Penrose, review of L. C. Dunn and Th. Dobzhansky, *Heredity, Race and Society,* revised edition (1952), *Annals of Eugenics,* XVII (1952–53), pp. 252–3.
3. J. P. Garlick, review of *Readings on Race,* ed. S. M. Garn (1960) and of Garn, *Human Races* (1961), *Annals of Human Genetics,* XXV (1961–62), pp. 169–70.
4. Ashley Montagu, 'The Concept of Race', *American Anthropologist,* LXIV (1962), p. 920.
5. *Man in Evolutionary Perspective,* ed. C. L. Brace and James Metress (New York etc., John Wiley & Sons, Inc., 1973), p. 341.
6. Montagu, *Man's most Dangerous Myth,* p. 3; Montagu, 'The Concept of Race', p. 927.
7. Frank B. Livingstone, 'On the Non-Existence of Human Races', *Current Anthropology,* III (1962), p. 279.
8. Julian Huxley, 'Clines: an Auxiliary Taxonomic Principle', *Nature,* CXLIII/3587 (30 July 1938), pp. 219–20.
9. Montagu, *Man's most Dangerous Myth,* p. 41.
10. Christopher Fyfe, 'The History of Racism in Britain – A Historian's Overview' (revised text of a talk given at the Africa Centre, London, 10 April 1984), p. 1. I am grateful to Fyfe for kindly sending me a copy of this text.

Chapter 11

1. Elizabeth Fox-Genovese and Eugene D. Genovese, *Fruits of Merchant Capital: Slavery and Bourgeois Property in the Rise and Expansion of Capitalism* (Oxford etc., Oxford University Press, 1983), pp. vii, 403 (italics added); cf. also Elsa V. Goveia, *A Study on the Historiography of the British West Indies to the End of the*

Nineteenth Century (México, Instituto Panamericano de Geografía e Historia, 1956), pp. 173–4.

2 F. O. Shyllon, *Black Slaves in Britain* (Oxford University Press for Institute of Race Relations, 1974), p. 21; P. Fryer, *Staying Power* (1984), pp. 115–16.

3. Shyllon, pp. 108–10; Fryer, pp. 124–5.

4 . J. G. Kemeys, *Free and Candid Reflections* (1783), pp. 72n., 79n.

5. See Fryer, p. 113.

6. See Fryer, pp. 148–50.

7. Maurice Cranston, *John Locke: a Biography* (Longmans, Green & Co., 1957), pp. 119–20, 153–6, 399ff.; Peter Laslett, 'John Locke, the Great Recoinage, and the Origins of the Board of Trade: 1695–1698', *William and Mary Quarterly*, 3rd ser. XIV (1957), pp. 370–402; Peter Laslett, Introduction to John Locke, *Two Treatises of Government*, second edition (Cambridge, University Press, 1967), pp. 39, 302–3n.

8. Harry M. Bracken, 'Philosophy and racism', *Philosophia*, VIII (1978–79), p. 243. See also H. M. Bracken, 'Essence, accident and race', *Hermathena*, no. 116 (Winter 1973), pp. 81–96.

9. David Hume, *Essays Moral, Political and Literary*, ed. T. H. Green and T. H. Grose (Darmstadt, Scientia Verlag Aalen, 1964), p. 252n.

10. Bracken, 'Philosophy and racism', p. 257.

11. See Fryer, pp. 158–60.

Chapter 12

1. *Spectator*, no. 1942 (16 September 1865), p. 1035.

2. Karl Pearson, *National Life from the Standpoint of Science* (Adam & Charles Black, 1901 [1900]).

3. L. P. Curtis, Jr., *Anglo-Saxons and Celts: A Study of Anti-Irish Prejudice in Victorian England* (Studies in British History and Culture, II, Bridgeport, Conn., Conference on British Studies at the University of Bridgeport, 1968), p. 121; Edward B. Snyder, 'The wild Irish: a study of some English satires against the Irish, Scots, and Welsh', *Modern Philology*, XVII/2 (April 1920), pp. 147–85.

4. *Imperialism*, ed. Philip D. Curtin (Macmillan, 1971), p. 1.

5. Bernard Porter, *The Lion's Share: A Short History of British Imperialism 1850–1970* (London & New York, Longman, 1975), p. 186.

6. Kenneth Robinson, *Dilemmas of Trusteeship: Aspects of British Colonial Policy Between the Wars* (Oxford University Press, 1965), p. 43.

7. *The last will and testament of Cecil John Rhodes: with elucidatory notes: to which are added some chapters describing the political and religious ideas of the testator*, ed. W. T. Stead (*Review of*

Reviews office, [1902]), p. 140.

8. *Parliamentary Debates*, 5th ser. vol. 150 (1922), col. 940.
9. Sir Harry Johnston, *The Backward Peoples and our Relations with Them* (Oxford University Press, 1920), p. 60.
10. Lord Milner, *The Nation and the Empire: Being a Collection of Speeches and Addresses* (Constable & Company Ltd., 1913), pp. xxxiii, 294.
11. Norman Angell, *The Unseen Assassins* (Hamish Hamilton, 1932), p. 221.
12. Porter, p. 46.
13. R. Hyam, *Britain's Imperial Century* (1976), p. 234.
14. Sydney H. Zebel, *Balfour: a Political Biography* (Cambridge, University Press, 1973), pp. 154, 155.
15. As quoted, *Speeches of Gopal Krishna Gokhale*, third edition (Madras, G. A. Nateson & Co., 1920), p. 451.
16. *Supplement to the Gazette of India*, no. 23 (4 June 1904), p. 937.
17. Anil Seal, *The Emergence of Indian Nationalism: Competition and Collaboration in the late Nineteenth Century* (Cambridge, University Press, 1968), p. 5.
18. Frances M. Mannsaker, 'East and west: Anglo-Indian racial attitudes as reflected in popular fiction, 1890–1914', *Victorian Studies*, XXIV (1980–81), pp. 50, 35.
19. Porter, p. 72; cf. David Beers Quinn, *The Elizabethans and the Irish* (Ithaca, NY, Cornell University Press for The Folger Shakespeare Library, 1966).
20. Porter, p. 180.
21. T[homas]. H[enry]. H[uxley]., 'Emancipation – black and white', *The Reader*, V/125 (20 May 1865), p. 561.
22. F. D. Lugard, *The Rise of our East African Empire* (1893), I, pp. 73–4.
23. H. L. Duff, *Nyasaland under the Foreign Office* (George Bell & Sons, 1903), p. 382. For the importance attached to maintaining the prestige of British officials in Nigeria, see F. K. Ekechi, *Missionary Enterprise and Rivalry in Igboland 1857–1914* (Cass Library of African Studies, General Studies no. 119, Frank Cass, 1971), p. 181.
24. Robert A. Huttenback, *Racism and Empire: White Settlers and Colored Immigrants in the British Self-Governing Colonies 1830–1910* (Ithaca & London, Cornell University Press, 1976), pp. 315–18.
25. Denis Judd, *Balfour and the British Empire: a study in imperial evolution 1874–1932* (London etc., Macmillan; New York, St Martin's Press, 1968), p. 195; Kenneth Young, *Arthur James Balfour: the Happy Life of the Politician, Prime Minister, Statesman and*

Philosopher 1848–1930 (G. Bell & Sons Ltd, 1963), p. 281; *Parliamentary Debates*, 5th ser. vol. 9 (1909), col. 1002.

26. Henry Drummond, *Tropical Africa* (Hodder & Stoughton, 1888), p. 4.
27. Duff, p. 383.
28. Frank Scudamore, *A Sheaf of Memories* (T. Fisher Unwin Ltd, 1925), p. 213.
29. Edward B. Tylor, *Primitive Culture: Researches into the Development of Mythology, Philosophy, Religion, Art, and Custom* (John Murray, 1871), p. 27.
30. Samuel White Baker, *The Albert N'yanza, Great Basin of the Nile, and Explorations of the Nile Sources* (Macmillan & Co., 1866), I, pp. 72, 78, 79, 164, 373, 241–2, 291.
31. G. W. Steevens, *The Land of the Dollar* (Edinburgh & London, William Blackwood & Sons, 1897), pp. 102, 104.
32. G. W. Steevens, *Egypt in 1898* (Edinburgh & London, William Blackwood & Sons, 1898), p. 11.
33. *The Milner Papers*, II, ed. C. Headlam (1933), p. 312.
34. H. A. C. Cairns, *Prelude to Imperialism* (1965), p. 95.
35. Lord Rosebery, *Questions of Empire: A Rectorial Address delivered before the Students of the University of Glasgow November the Sixteenth Nineteen Hundred* (Arthur L. Humphreys, 1900), p. 32. I owe this quotation to Christopher Fyfe, 'White Authority in Colonial Africa' (paper presented at a symposium on 'Authority and Legitimacy in Africa', University of Stirling, 23 May 1986), p. 14, and am grateful to Fyfe for sending me a copy of that paper.

Chapter 13

1. Eric Williams, 'The historical background of race relations in the Caribbean', in *Miscelánea de estudios dedicados a Fernando Ortiz por sus discipulos, colegas y amigos* (Havana, 1955–57), III, p. 1541; E. Williams, *British Historians and the West Indies* (1966), p. 46.
2. Williams, *British Historians*, pp. 166, 168.
3. Williams, *British Historians*, p. 46.
4. J. W. Burrow, *A Liberal Descent: Victorian Historians and the English Past* (Cambridge University Press, 1981), p. 300.
5. *Selections from Educational Records*, pt i, 1781–1839, ed. H. Sharp (Calcutta, Superintendent Government Printing, India, 1920), p. 110.
6. John Kenyon, *The History Men: The Historical Profession in England since the Renaissance* (Weidenfeld & Nicolson, 1983), p. 123.
7. Burrow, pp. 233, 231.
8. James Anthony Froude, *Oceana, or England and her Colonies*

(Longmans, Green, & Co., 1886), p. 11.

9. James Anthony Froude, *The English in the West Indies, or The Bow of Ulysses* (Longmans, Green, & Co., 1888), pp. 235, 348, 161, 286. The private journal Froude kept while in the Caribbean referred to his seeing 'swarms of niggers', 'all of them perfectly happy, without a notion of morality'. He added: 'Niggerdom perfect happiness' (as quoted by Herbert Paul, *The Life of Froude* (Sir Isaac Pitman & Sons, Ltd, 1905), p. 357.
10. Kenyon, p. 55.
11. Burrow, pp. 188–9, 191, 204.
12. W. R. W. Stephens, *The Life and Letters of Edward A. Freeman* (London & New York, Macmillan & Co., 1895), II, pp. 242, 234, 236–7.
13. Kenyon, pp. 149, 153.
14. Williams, *British Historians*, p. 78.
15. William Stubbs, *Seventeen Lectures on the Study of Medieval and Modern History and Kindred Subjects* (Oxford, Clarendon Press, 1886), pp. 239–40.
16. Kenyon, p. 125.
17. [J. D. Acton], 'Political thoughts on the Church', *The Rambler*, n.s. XI (1859), p. 43, reprinted in John Emerich Dalberg-Acton, *The History of Freedom and other Essays*, ed. John Neville Figgis & Reginald Vere Laurence (Macmillan & Co., Limited, 1907), p. 204.
18. [J. D. Acton], 'Mr. Goldwin Smith's Irish history', *The Rambler*, n.s. VI (1861–62), p. 197, reprinted in Dalberg-Acton, *The History of Freedom*, pp. 240–1.
19. James Mill, *The History of British India* (Baldwin, Cradock, & Joy, 1817), I, p. 99.
20. [Acton], 'Mr. Goldwin Smith's Irish history', p. 197, reprinted in Dalberg-Acton, *The History of Freedom*, p. 241.
21. [J. D. Acton], 'Nationality', *Home and Foreign Review*, I (1862), p. 17, reprinted in Dalberg-Acton, *The History of Freedom*, p. 290.
22. John Emerich Dalberg-Acton, *Historical Essays & Studies*, ed. J. N. Figgis & R. V. Laurence (Macmillan & Co., Limited, 1907), p. 135.
23. Maurice Todhunter, 'Sir John Seeley', *Westminster Review*, CXLV (1896), p. 506.
24. Herbert A. L. Fisher, 'Sir John Seeley', *Fortnightly Review*, n.s. LX (1896), p. 191.
25. Peter Burroughs, 'John Robert Seeley and British Imperial History', *Journal of Imperial and Commonwealth History*, I (1972–73), pp. 206–7.
26. J. R. Seeley, *The Expansion of England: Two Courses of Lectures*

(Macmillan & Co., 1883), pp. 261, 252.

27. Williams, *British Historians*, p. 152. Their 'blatant' prejudices are also referred to in L. P. Curtis, Jr., *Anglo-Saxons and Celts* (1968), p. 89.
28. Hugh Edward Egerton, *British Colonial Policy in the XXth Century* (Methuen & Co. Ltd, 1922), pp. 193, 228, 173.
29. Arthur Bryant, *English Saga (1840–1940)* (Collins with Eyre & Spottiswoode, 1940), p. 266.
30. James Rodway, *History of British Guiana, from the Year 1668 to the Present Time* (Georgetown, Demerara, J. Thomson, 1891–94), III, pp. 88, 272–3.
31. A. Caldecott, *The Church in the West Indies* (Society for Promoting Christian Knowledge, 1898), p. 195.
32. W. P. Livingstone, *Black Jamaica: a Study in Evolution* (Sampson Low, Marston, & Company Limited, 1899), pp. 31–2, 15.
33. Dr R. C. Majumdar, Preface to *British Paramountcy and Indian Renaissance*, pt 1, ed. Majumdar (The History and Culture of the Indian People, IX, Bombay, Bharatiya Vidya Bhavan, 1963), p. xxv.
34. Edward Thompson & G. T. Garratt, *Rise and Fulfilment of British Rule in India* (Macmillan & Co., Limited, 1934), p. 665.
35. Joan Leopold, 'British applications of the Aryan theory of race to India, 1850–1870', *English Historical Review*, LXXXIX (1974), p. 598.
36. *Listener*, 28 November 1963, p. 871.
37. *Guardian*, 14 January 1986, p. 21.
38. J. A. Hobson, *Imperialism: a Study* (James Nisbet & Co., Limited, 1902), pp. 229–30.
39. Valerie E. Chancellor, *History for their Masters: Opinion in the English History Textbook: 1800–1914* (Adams & Dart, 1970), pp. 122–4, 127, 137.
40. *The Class History of England* (London etc., Cassell & Company, Limited, [1884]), p. 400.
41. *The World and its People: Africa: With Special Reference to British Possessions* (London, Edinburgh, & New York, Thomas Nelson & Sons, 1903), pp. 18–19.
42. C. R. L. Fletcher & Rudyard Kipling, *A School History of England* (Oxford, Clarendon Press, 1911), p. 240.
43. J. M. MacKenzie, *Propaganda and Empire* (1984), p. 179.
44. David Killingray, 'African history in the classroom', *Teaching History*, no. 17 (February 1977), p. 7.
45. Brian Street, 'Anthropology Outside the Classroom', *Journal of the*

Anthropological Society of Oxford, VI/1 (Hilary 1975), pp. 58, 59. For useful surveys of ethnocentric and racist bias in teaching materials, see: Stephen Hatch, 'Coloured People in School Textbooks', *Race*, IV/1 (November 1962), pp. 63–72; Frank Glendinning, 'Racial stereotypes in history textbooks', *Race Today*, III/2 (February 1971), pp. 52–4; Dave Hicks, *Images of the World: An Introduction to Bias in Teaching Materials* (Occasional Paper No. 2, Department for Education in Developing Countries & Centre for Multicultural Education, University of London Institute of Education, 1980); David Hicks, 'Bias in school books: messages from the ethnocentric curriculum', in *The School in the Multicultural Society*, ed. Alan James & Robert Jeffcoate (Harper & Row Ltd, 1981), pp. 163–77; and David R. Wright, 'What do pupils learn about race?', *Education Journal*, VI/1 (April 1984), pp. 1–5.

46. H. John Field, *Toward a Programme of Imperial Life; The British Empire at the Turn of the Century* (Contributions in Comparative Colonial Studies, no. 9, Westport, Conn., Greenwood Press, 1982), pp. 104, 112.
47. Patrick A. Duane, 'Boys' literature and the idea of race: 1870–1900', *Wascana Review*, (spring 1977), p. 85. I am grateful to the British Library for obtaining a photocopy of this paper for me.
48. Jake W. Spidle, 'Victorian juvenilia and the image of the black African', *Journal of Popular Culture*, IX (1975–76), pp. 57–61.
49. Roy Turnbaugh, 'Images of empire: George Alfred Henty and John Buchan', *Journal of Popular Culture*, IX (1975–76), p. 735.
50. Duane, pp. 85–8, 102–3. See also Brian V. Street, *The Savage in Literature: Representations of 'Primitive' Society in English Fiction 1858–1920* (London & Boston, Routledge & Kegan Paul, 1975).
51. Cf. David Milner, *Children and Race* (Harmondsworth, Penguin Books Ltd, 1975), pp. 70, 215. A revised edition of this book appeared as *Children and Race: Ten Years On* (Ward Lock Educational, 1983).
52. Bob Dixon, *Catching Them Young 1: Sex, Race and Class in Children's Fiction* (Pluto Press, 1977), pp. 94–127. See also: Milner, *Children and Race* (1975), pp. 215–32; Sarah Goodman Zimet, *Print and Prejudice* (Hodder & Stoughton for the United Kingdom Reading Association, 1976); and *Racism and Sexism in Children's Books*, ed. Judith Stinton (Writers and Readers, 1979).

Part III

Chapter 14

1. Darold D. Wax, 'Negro resistance to the early American slave trade', *Journal of Negro History,* LI (1966), pp. 6–7, 9–10. For revolts by slaves held on the Senegambia island of Gorée, see [Antoine Edme] P[runeau]. D[e]. P[ommegorge]., *Description de la Nigritie* (Amsterdam & Paris, chez Maradan, 1789), pp. 102ff.
2. Daniel P. Mannix and Malcolm Cowley, *Black Cargoes: A History of the Atlantic Slave Trade 1518–1865* (Longmans, 1963), pp. 108–11.
3. Michael Craton, *Testing the Chains: Resistance to Slavery in the British West Indies* (Ithaca & London, Cornell University Press, 1982), p. 24.
4. Craton, p. 40, citing the journals of Thomas Thistlewood; the same passage is incorrectly transcribed in O. A. Sherrard, *Freedom from Fear: The Slave and his Emancipation* (Bodley Head, 1959), p. 88.
5. Michael Craton & Garry Greenland, *Searching for the Invisible Man: Slaves and Plantation Life in Jamaica* (Cambridge, Mass. & London, Harvard University Press, 1978), p. 245.
6. For this paragraph, see Orlando Patterson, *The Sociology of Slavery: An Analysis of the Origins, Development and Structure of Negro Slave Society in Jamaica* (Macgibbon & Kee, 1967), pp. 260–83.
7. Craton, pp. 335–9.
8. Orlando Patterson, 'Slavery and slave revolts: a socio-historical analysis of the First Maroon War Jamaica, 1655–1740', *Social and Economic Studies,* XIX (1970), p. 289.
9. Craton, pp. 108–9; *Great newes from the Barbadoes: or, A True and Faithful account of the Grand Conspiracy of The Negroes against the English: and The Happy Discovery of the same* (L. Curtis, 1676), p. 3.
10. Reproduced in Craton, p. 111.
11. Craton, pp. 111–14.
12. John Atkins, *A voyage to Guinea, Brasil, and the West-Indies; In His Majesty's Ships, the Swallow and Weymouth* (Caesar Ward & Richard Chandler, 1735), p. 245. The word 'maroon' is derived, through the French *marron,* from the Spanish *cimarrón,* a runaway slave.
13. As quoted by Craton, p. 85.
14. As quoted by Patterson, *Sociology of Slavery,* p. 270.
15. Patterson, 'Slavery and slave revolts', pp. 289–325, Craton, pp. 67–96.

16. Lucille Mathurin [Mair], *The Rebel Woman in the British West Indies during Slavery* (Kingston, Institute of Jamaica for the Afro-Caribbean Institute of Jamaica, 1975), pp. 34–7; Patterson, 'Slavery and slave revolts', p. 302. See also Alan Tuelon, 'Nanny - Maroon Chieftainess', *Caribbean Quarterly*, XIX/4 (December 1973), pp. 20–7. And, for the part played by women in black resistance generally, see Barbara Bush, '"The Family Tree Is Not Cut": Women and Cultural Resistance in Slave Family Life in the British Caribbean', in *In Resistance: Studies in African, Caribbean, and Afro-American History*, ed. Gary Y. Okihiro (Amherst, University of Massachusetts Press, 1986), pp. 117–32, and Rosalyn Terborg-Penn, 'Black Women in Resistance: A Cross-Cultural Perspective', in *In Resistance*, ed. Okihiro, pp. 188–209.
17. David Barry Gaspar, 'The Antigua Slave Conspiracy of 1736: A Case Study of the Origins of Collective Resistance', *William and Mary Quarterly*, 3rd ser. XXXV/2 (April 1978), p. 317.
18. Gaspar, pp. 308-23; Craton, pp. 120–4.
19. Craton, p. 125.
20. Bryan Edwards, *The History, Civil and Commercial, of The British Colonies in the West Indies* (John Stockdale, 1793–1801), II, p. 64.
21. Edwards, II, p. 65. For the 1760–61 uprising in Jamaica, see: C. Roy Reynolds, 'Tacky and the great slave rebellion of 1760', *Jamaica Journal*, VI/2 (June 1972), pp. 5–8; Carl A. Lane, 'Concerning Jamaica's 1760 slave rebellions', *Jamaica Journal*, VII/4 (December 1973), pp. 2–4; Craton, pp. 129–38.
22. As quoted by Craton, p. 172.
23. Craton, pp. 172–9.
24. Craton, p. 224.
25. Lennox Honychurch, *The Dominica story: A History of the Island* ([Dominica] 1975), pp. 54–6.
26. As quoted by Craton, p. 225.
27. Craton, pp. 141–5, 224–9.
28. Craton, p. 164.
29. Craton, p. 189.
30. Craton, p. 109.
31. For the Fédon uprising in Grenada, see Craton, pp. 183–90, 207–10.
32. Craton, pp. 195–204.
33. Honychurch, pp. 62–4; Craton, pp. 231–2.
34. Craton, pp. 254–66.
35. Joshua Bryant, *Account of an Insurrection of the Negro Slaves in the Colony of Demerara* (Georgetown, 1824); Eric Williams, 'The

historical background of British Guiana's problems', *Journal of Negro History*, XXX (1945), pp. 374–5; Cecil Northcott, *Slavery's Martyr: John Smith of Demerara and The Emancipation Movement 1817–24* (Epworth Press, 1976); Craton, pp. 267–90.

36. W. J. Gardner, *A History of Jamaica from its Discovery by Christopher Columbus to the Present Time* (Eliot Stock, 1873), p. 261; Craton, p. 294.
37. Craton, p. 291.
38. John Howard Hinton, *Memoir of William Knibb, Missionary in Jamaica* (Houlston & Stoneman, 1847), pp. 112–13.
39. Eugene D. Genovese, *From Rebellion to Revolution: Afro-American Slave Revolts in the Making of the Modern World* (Baton Rouge & London, Louisiana State University Press, 1979), p. 103.
40. Mary Reckord, 'The Jamaica slave rebellion of 1831', *Past & Present*, 40 (July 1968), p. 113.
41. Craton, p. 303.
42. Henry Bleby, *Death struggles of slavery: being a narrative of facts and incidents which occurred in a British colony, during the two years immediately preceding negro emancipation* (Hamilton, Adams, & Co., 1853), pp. 31–2.
43. Craton, p. 314.
44. Bleby, pp. 29–30, 115, 116. For the 1831–32 rising in Jamaica, see: Reckord, pp. 108–25; Barry Chevannes, 'Revival and black struggle', *Savacou*, 5 (June 1971), pp. 30–2; Craton, pp. 291–321.
45. Richard Frucht, 'Emancipation and revolt in the West Indies: St Kitts, 1834', *Science & Society*, XXXIX (1975), pp. 199–214.
46. Sir Alan Burns, *History of the British West Indies* (George Allen & Unwin Ltd, 1954), p. 5.
47. Eric Williams, *Capitalism & Slavery* (Chapel Hill, University of North Carolina Press, 1944), p. 201.

Chapter 15

1. M. Craton, *Testing the Chains* (1982), pp. 324–5.
2. Frank Cundall, *Political and Social Disturbances in the West Indies: a Brief Account and Bibliography* (Kingston, Educational Supply Co. for Institute of Jamaica; London, H. Sotheran & Co.; 1906), pp. 4–5. Cundall also includes the 1837 mutiny in Trinidad by soldiers of the First West India Regiment.
3. Raymond M. Cooke, 'The Historian as Underdog: Eric Williams and the British Empire', *The Historian*, XXXIII (1970–71), p. 597.
4. Queen Victoria's reply is quoted in full in Lord [Sydney Haldane] Olivier, *The Myth of Governor Eyre* (Hogarth Press,

1933), pp. 145–6.

5. As quoted by Olivier, p. 250.
6. For the 1865 Jamaican rebellion, see, besides Olivier's book, the following: *Report of the Jamaica Royal Commission, 1866* (Parliamentary Papers, 1866, XXX, XXXI); Douglas Hall, *Free Jamaica 1838–1865: An Economic History* (Caribbean Ser. 1, New Haven, Yale University Press, 1959), pp. 242–54; Mavis Christine Campbell, *The Dynamics of Change in a Slave Society: A Sociopolitical History of the Free Coloreds of Jamaica, 1800–1865* (Rutherford, etc., Farleigh Dickinson University Press; London, Associated University Presses; 1976), pp. 314ff. See also the references in P. Fryer, *Staying Power* (1984), p. 534 nn. 60, 63.
7. For the 1876 Barbados uprising, see: *Papers relating to the late disturbances in Barbados* (C. 1539, Parliamentary Papers, 1876, LIII); *Further papers relating to the late disturbances in Barbados* (C. 1559, Parliamentary Papers, 1876, LIII); Bruce Hamilton, *Barbados & the Confederation Question 1871–1885* (Crown Agents for Oversea Governments & Administrations, for Government of Barbados, 1956), pp. 71ff.; James Pope-Hennessy, *Verandah: Some Episodes in the Crown Colonies 1867–1889* (George Allen & Unwin Ltd, 1964), pp. 161ff.
8. Eric Williams, *History of the People of Trinidad and Tobago* (André Deutsch, 1964), pp. 179ff.; Bridget Brereton, *A History of Modern Trinidad 1783–1962* (Kingston etc., Heinemann, 1981), pp. 149–51.
9. Ashton Chase, *A History of Trade Unionism in Guyana 1900 to 1961* (Ruimveldt, New Guyana Co. Ltd, [1964]), pp. 20ff.; Walter Rodney, *A History of the Guyanese Working People, 1881–1905* (Kingston etc., Heinemann Educational Books, 1981), pp. 190ff.
10. W. F. Elkins, 'Black Power in the British West Indies: the Trinidad Longshoremen's Strike of 1919', *Science & Society*, XXXIII (1969), pp. 71–5; Tony Martin, 'Revolutionary upheaval in Trinidad, 1919: views from British and American sources', *Journal of Negro History*, LVIII (1973), pp. 313–26; Brereton, pp. 157–64.
11. Eric Williams, *From Columbus to Castro: The History of the Caribbean 1492–1969* (André Deutsch, 1970), pp. 473–4; F. A. Hoyos, *The Rise of West Indian Democracy: The Life & Times of Sir Grantley Adams* ([Bridgetown?], Advocate Press, 1963), p. 62.
12. Peter D. Ashdown, 'Antonio Soberanis and the 1934-1935 disturbances in Belize', *Belizean Studies*, V/4 (July 1977), pp. 1–11; V/5 (September 1977), pp. 16–28; VI/2 (March 1978), pp. 12–19; VI/3 (May 1978), pp. 7–12; VI/4 (July 1978), pp. 8–15.

13. Brereton, p. 171.
14. Brereton, pp. 176–85.
15. *Report of the Commission appointed to enquire into The Disturbances which took place in Barbados on the 27th July 1937 and subsequent days* [Bridgetown? 1937]; Hoyos, *The Rise of West Indian Democracy*, pp. 62–7; Dr Francis Mark, *The History of the Barbados Workers' Union* ([Bridgetown], Barbados Workers' Union, [*c.* 1966]), pp. 1–8; The Honourable F. A. Hoyos, *Barbados: A History from the Amerindians to Independence* (Macmillan, 1978), pp. 206–10. The Barbados Progressive League was at first called the Barbados Labour Party.
16. O. W. Phelps, 'Rise of the Labour Movement in Jamaica', *Social and Economic Studies*, IX (1960), pp. 417–35; K. W. J. Post, 'The Politics of Protest in Jamaica, 1938: Some Problems of Analysis and Conceptualization', *Social and Economic Studies*, XVIII (1969), pp. 374–90; Ken Post, *Arise ye Starvelings: The Jamaican Labour Rebellion of 1938 and its Aftermath* (Institute of Social Studies Ser. on the Development of Societies, III, The Hague etc., Martinus Nijhoff, 1978), esp. pp. 238, 276–84. There is an impressionistic but vivid account of the Kingston events in William J. Makin, *Caribbean Nights* (Robert Hale Limited, 1939), pp. 60ff.
17. Chase, pp. 87–90; Vere T. Daly, *A Short History of the Guyanese People* (Macmillan, 1975), p. 294.

Chapter 16

1. S. B. Chaudhuri, *Civil Disturbances during the British Rule in India (1765–1857)* (Calcutta, The World Press Ltd, 1955), pp. xxii, 198.
2. Rai Sahib Jamini Mohan Ghosh, *Sannyasi and Fakir Raiders in Bengal* (Calcutta, Bengal Secretariat Book Depot, 1930), pp. 50ff.
3. E. Bell, *Memoir of General John Briggs* (1885), p. 24.
4. *British Paramountcy and Indian Renaissance*, pt 1, ed. R. C. Majumdar and others (The History and Culture of the Indian People, IX, Bombay, Bharatiya Vidya Bhavan, 1963), p. 406. For the armed struggle before 1857, see also: R. C. Majumdar, *History of the freedom movement in India* (Calcutta, Firma K. L. Mukhopadhyay, 1962–63), I, pp. 48–143; Narahari Kaviraj, 'Spontaneous peasant risings as a problem of historiography', in *Marxism and Indology*, ed. Debiprasad Chattopadhyaya (Calcutta & New Delhi, K. P. Bagchi & Co., 1981), pp. 137–52.
5. Eric Stokes, 'Traditional resistance movements and Afro-Asian nationalism: the context of the 1857 mutiny rebellion in India', *Past*

& Present, no. 48 (August 1970), p. 110.

6. Cf. Nandalal Chatterji, 'A Century of India's Freedom Struggle', *Journal of Indian History*, XXXV (1957), p. 224.
7. Sashi Bhusan Chaudhuri, *Civil Rebellion in the Indian Mutinies (1857–1859)* (Calcutta, The World Press Private Ltd, 1957), p. 269.
8. B. Mark Thornhill, *The Personal Adventures and Experiences of a Magistrate during the Rise, Progress, and Suppression of the Indian Mutiny* (John Murray, 1884), p. 178.
9. W. H. Fitchett, *The Tale of the Great Mutiny* (Smith, Elder. & Co., 1901), p. 49.
10. Colonel G. B. Malleson, *History of the Indian Mutiny, 1857–1858: commencing from the Close of the Second Volume of Sir John Kaye's History of the Sepoy War* (William H. Allen & Co., 1878-80), III, p. 205.
11. [William Wotherspoon Ireland, M.D.], *History of the siege of Delhi by an officer who served there: with a sketch of the leading events in the Punjaub connected with the great rebellion of 1857* (Edinburgh, Adam & Charles Black, 1861), pp. 159–60, 256.
12. C. W. Dilke, *Greater Britain* (1868), II, p. 225.
13. John William Kaye, *A History of the Sepoy War in India: 1857–58* (W. H. Allen & Co., 1864–76), II, pp. 170, 235–7.
14. G. O. Trevelyan, *The Competition Wallah* (London & Cambridge, Macmillan & Co., 1864), p. 284; Kaye, II, p. 400. Colonel John Nicholson wanted a special Act passed legalizing the torture of those who had killed British women and children; he wanted them flayed alive, impaled, or burnt.
15. R. M. Coopland, *A lady's escape from Gwalior and life in the fort of Agra during the mutinies of 1857* (Smith, Elder, & Co., 1859), p. 233.
16. Lieut. Vivian Dering Majendie, *Up among the Pandies: or, A Year's Service in India* (London & New York, Routledge, Warne, & Routledge, 1859), pp. 186–7; William Howard Russell, *My Diary in India, in the Year 1858–9* (Routledge, Warne, & Routledge, 1860), I, pp. 301–2.
17. Stokes, p. 113; cf. Nandalal Chatterji, 'The Cult of Violence and India's Freedom Movement', *Journal of Indian History*, XXXV (1957), p. 1.
18. Blair B. Kling, *The Blue Mutiny: The Indigo Disturbances in Bengal 1859–1862* (Philadelphia, University of Pennsylvania Press, 1966),p. 60.
19. Kling, pp. 222, 8. For the Blue Mutiny, see also *British Paramountcy and Indian Renaissance*, pt 1, ed. Majumdar and others, pp. 926–37.

20. Sir William Wedderburn, Bart., *Allan Octavian Hume, C.B.: 'Father of the Indian National Congress': 1829 to 1912* (T. Fisher Unwin, 1913), p. 82; *British Paramountcy and Indian Renaissance*, pt 1, ed. Majumdar and others, pp. 938–40.
21. Wedderburn, p. 77.
22. Cf. *British Paramountcy and Indian Renaissance*, pt 2, ed. R. C. Majumdar (1965), p. 570.
23. F. M. De Mello, *The Indian National Congress: An Historical Sketch* (Oxford University Press, 1934), p. 2; Briton Martin, Jr, *New India, 1885: British Official Policy and the Emergence of the Indian National Congress* (Berkeley & Los Angeles, University of California Press, 1969), pp. 328–9; John R. McLaine, *Indian Nationalism and the Early Congress* (Princeton, N.J., Princeton University Press, 1977), p. 117.
24. For Aurobindo Ghose, see Leonard A. Gordon, *Bengal: The Nationalist Movement 1876–1940* (New York & London, Columbia University Press, 1974), pp. 101–34. For Lajpat Rai, see Daniel Argov, *Moderates and Extremists in the Indian Nationalist Movement 1883–1920: With Special Reference to Surendranath Banerjea and Lajpat Rai* (Asia Publishing House, 1967), esp. pp. 59–94.
25. A. R. Desai, *Social Background of Indian Nationalism*, 5th edition (Sangam Books, 1984 reprint), p. 372.
26. Ram Gopal, *How India Struggled for Freedom (A Political History)*[Bombay, The Book Centre (Private) Ltd; London, Frederick Muller Ltd; 1967], p. 436.
27. Majumdar, *History of the Freedom Movement*, III, pp. 649–50.
28. Majumdar, *History of the Freedom Movement*, III, pp. 657–8. For the 1942 uprising, see also [R. C. Majumdar and P. N. Chopra], 'The Outbreak of 1942', in *Struggle for Freedom*, ed. R. C. Majumdar (The History and Culture of the Indian People, XI, Bombay, Bharatiya Vidya Bhavan, 1969), pp. 651–81.
29. V. P. Menon, *The Transfer of Power in India* (Bombay etc., Orient Longmans, 1957), pp. 228–9; *Constitutional Relations between Britain and India: The Transfer of Power 1942–7*, VI: The post-war phase, ed. Nicholas Mansergh (HMSO, 1976), esp. pp. 1071–2, 1079–84, 1234.

Conclusion

1. Harold Macmillan, *At the End of the Day 1961–1963* (Macmillan, 1973), pp. 73–4.
2. PRO CAB 128/25/333.
3. PRO CAB 128/25/368–9. R. A. Butler, Chancellor of the Exchequer, reported in February 1954 that 'It would not be possible to revise

the Regulations in such a way as to exclude coloured candidates effectively from eligibility for established Civil Service appointment without coming into the open about it in one way or another'; and that 'any discrimination ... would either have to be, or become, overt and would involve difficulties of principle out of all proportion to any practical advantage which the Civil Service might derive from it' ('Recruitment of Coloured Persons to the Civil Service', Memorandum by the Chancellor of the Exchequer, PRO CAB 129/65/158–60).

4. W. H. Hardman, memorandum dated 4 September 1953, in PRO LAB 8/1898. I am grateful to John Spencer for this reference.
5. As quoted by Zig Layton-Henry, *The Politics of Race in Britain* (George Allen & Unwin, 1984), p. 32.
6. 'Coloured People seeking Employment in the United Kingdom: Extract from Note by the Home Office Dated 11th July, 1953' and supplementary material, in PRO LAB 8/1898.
7. 'Employment of Coloured People', Memorandum by the Secretary of State for the Home Department and Minister for Welsh Affairs, PRO CAB 129/65/147–9; 'Report of the Committee on the Social and Economic Problems Arising from the Growing Influx into the United Kingdom of Coloured Workers from Other Commonwealth Countries', Appendix, PRO CAB 129/77/10-17.
8. 'The Employment Position of Coloured Workers': Note by the Ministry of Labour and National Service, 28 September 1953, in PRO LAB 8/1898.
9. 'Colonial Immigrants', Report of the Committee of Ministers, PRO CAB 129/81/167-71.
10. 'Colonial Immigrants', PRO CAB 129/81/167-71.
11. Here and in what follows I have made use of Edward Pilkington's paper 'The Great Immigration Swindle', a copy of which he kindly sent me before its publication in *Voice*, 21 February 1987.
12. PRO CAB 129/65/147–9.
13. 'Colonial Immigrants', Memorandum by Secretary of State for the Home Department, PRO CAB 129/72/17–18.
14. 'Colonial Immigrants', Memorandum by Secretary of State for Commonwealth Relations, PRO CAB 129/72/23–4.
15. 'Colonial Immigrants', Memorandum by Secretary of State for the Home Department, PRO CAB 129/75/178–80.
16. Pilkington, 'The Great Immigration Swindle', f. 5.
17. Michael and Ann Dummett, 'The role of government in Britain's racial crisis', in John Downing and others, *Justice First*, ed. Lewis Donnelly (London & Sydney, Sheed & Ward, 1969), p. 78.

18. Gordon K. Lewis, *Slavery, Imperialism, and Freedom: Studies in English Radical Thought* (New York & London, Monthly Review Press, 1978), pp. 317–18.
19. As quoted, *Daily Mail*, 31 January 1978, p. 1.
20. Cf. *Searchlight*, no. 116 (February 1985), p. 3.
21. *Searchlight*, no. 109 (July 1984), p. 20.
22. *Searchlight*, no. 138 (December 1986), p. 15; no. 139 (January 1987), p. 19.
23. As quoted, *Policing London*, no. 2 (September 1982).
24. *Policing London*, no. 4 (November 1982).
25. David J. Smith and Jeremy Gray, *Police and People in London: The PSI Report* (Gower, 1985), pp. 388–9, 389, 404, 390, 392, 393, 599.
26. *Policing London*, no. 1 (July/August 1982).
27. *Searchlight*, no. 130 (April 1986), p. 17.
28. *Searchlight*, no. 130 (April 1986), p. 17.
29. *Racial Attacks: Report of a Home Office Study* (Home Office, 1981), pp. 10–11, 12, 16, 35, 36.
30. *Searchlight*, no. 94 (April 1983), p. 11.
31. *Searchlight*, no. 103 (January 1984), p. 18.
32. *Searchlight*, no. 115 (January 1985), pp. 10–11.
33. *Searchlight*, no. 120 (June 1985), p. 17.
34. *Searchlight*, no. 129 (March 1986), p. 4.
35. *Searchlight*, no. 134 (August 1986), p. 12.
36. *Searchlight*, no. 137 (November 1986), p. 5.
37. *Searchlight*, no. 143 (May 1987), p. 19.
38. *Searchlight*, no. 144 (June 1987), pp. 5, 7.
39. *Searchlight*, no. 146 (August 1987), p. 6.
40. *Searchlight*, no. 135 (September 1986), pp. 5, 19.

Suggestions for Further Reading

Whatever corrections of detail may be necessary after more than 40 years, Eric Williams's *Capitalism & Slavery* (Chapel Hill, University of North Carolina Press, 1944; third impression, André Deutsch, 1972) is still the best introduction to the earliest phase of British colonialism. For the nineteenth century, see first of all Walter Rodney, *How Europe Underdeveloped Africa* (Bogle-L'Ouverture Publications, 1978). Informative general treatments of European capitalism's 'underdevelopment' of its colonies and semi-colonies will be found in Paul A. Baran, *The Political Economy of Growth* (John Calder, 1957), and Andre Gunder Frank, *Capitalism and Underdevelopment in Latin America: Historical Studies of Chile and Brazil* (Harmondsworth, Penguin Books Ltd, 1969). For further information on the history of English racism see Chapter 7 of Peter Fryer, *Staying Power: The History of Black People in Britain* (Pluto Press, 1984), pp. 133–90. The best brief overview of black resistance is Jagdish Gundara, 'Lessons from History for Black Resistance in Britain', in *Race, Migration and Schooling*, ed. John Tierney (Holt, Rinehart and Winston, 1982), pp. 44–57. The serious student will also find indispensable a collection of essays entitled *In Resistance: Studies in African, Caribbean, and Afro-American History*, ed. Gary Y. Okihiro (Amherst, University of Massachusetts Press, 1986). This excellent volume pays special attention to the part played by women in black resistance.

Some of the notes above contain reading lists on specific topics; these notes are identified in the index under the rubric 'further reading'.

Index